CREATION
IN CRISIS?

Alex MacDonald

Christian Focus Publications

Scripture references, unless otherwise indicated, are from the New International Version, published by Hodder and Stoughton.

© 1992 Alex MacDonald

ISBN 1 871 676 86X

Published by
Christian Focus Publications Ltd
Geanies House, Fearn, Ross-shire,
IV20 1TW, Great Britain.

Printed and bound in Great Britain by
Cox & Wyman Ltd, Reading

Cover design
by
Seoris N. McGillivray.

CONTENTS

INTRODUCTION

One of the remarkable features in the last quarter of the twentieth century is the rise of the Green movement. The impact of various environmental pressure groups on political parties has been remarkable. The success of the Greens in presenting their case in the media has been phenomenal. So much so that most people seem to be convinced that there is such a thing as a major ecological crisis. While I am aware that there are scientists who are more cautious or even dispute the doom-laden forecasts, in this book I am proceeding on the assumption that there is a crisis. This is for three reasons. First, I am no expert in ecology and I have to rely on what most experts seem to be saying. Second, at a common-sense level I can see that if you catch all the herring in the sea, they will become extinct; if you cut down all the trees on hillsides, the soil will wash away never to return; and if you pour millions of gallons of poisons into rivers and oceans, you will kill fish and maybe people too.

My third reason is the most urgent and is the reason why I am writing this book. I believe the real crisis lies not in the various environmental disasters, real, potential or imaginary, but in the human response to these perceived disasters. There is a crisis in confidence in old ways of thinking. Included in these old ways is Christianity. It is perceived by many to be too man-centred to be of any use in solving the ecological crisis. What we need, they say, is a world-view that will give us a sense of oneness with nature and they look to the East and to the West's pagan past, blended with the theories of modern physics and biology, for such a new spirituality.

The crisis, therefore, concerns the very concept of creation. And the choice is no longer between the clear alternatives of the Christian view that God has created the universe and the materialist view that the universe has simply developed due to impersonal forces. There is a third voice being heard ever more strongly, which says we are one with the universe and we are creating it. It has been called a world-view just being born. It is usually called New Age thinking.

The original meaning of 'crisis' is judgement, and we do indeed stand at a momentous place of judgement. We must decide which world-view we must adopt, not only to deal with the ecological crisis, but to deal with every crisis, personal, ethical or political. The world-view adopted in the West at the end of the second millennium will have fateful consequences for the whole world as it will control the science and technology which the whole world desires.

I believe that New Age thinking will fail to produce the promised utopia, just as materialism, whether Communist or Western, has failed, because none of these holds that we are answerable to a higher authority than ourselves, and none of them has any power to change that intractable thing - evil in the heart of man.

CREATION IN CRISIS?

It is my conviction that only historic, biblical Christianity has the answer to all our crises, including the ecological crisis, because only the Bible shows us that we are answerable to the unlimited, personal God who has created us and to whom the universe belongs. Only this Word of God reveals to us the origin of evil in the world and the cosmic consequences of the redemptive act of God in Jesus Christ. As ever, you are called upon to choose. 'Choose for yourselves this day whom you will serve, whether the gods your forefathers served beyond the River, or the gods of the Amorites, in whose land you are living. But as for me and my household, we will serve the LORD' (Joshua 24:15). As we enter the third millennium, will we be plunging the world into a new dark age or will we be laying the foundation of a new creation?

PART 1

MAN WHO MADE
THE WORLD
A DESERT

CHAPTER 1

LAND IS LIFE

The surgeon Paul Brand is widely known and rightly respected for his pioneering work in the treatment of leprosy in India. What is perhaps not so well known is that he cares passionately about the earth too. He grew up in the hills of South India where his parents were missionaries, and he tells of one boyhood experience there that left an indelible impression on his mind.

One day he was playing with his friends in the rice fields. These fields were not all the same level, but were terraced along the courses of the streams that ran down from the hills. Each terrace was bordered by an earthen dam topped by a grassy path, and every few feet along the path there were little channels cut to allow the water to trickle down to the next terrace. These rice fields, which provided an important part of the staple diet of the people, were the work of generations. They were also a favourite playground for the children especially when the water was full of frogs and little fish!

This day the boys were trying to catch frogs, churning up the mud and flattening the rice plants in the process, when they were caught by Tata, the old man who was keeper of the dams.

He stared down at the churned-up mud and flattened young rice plants in the corner where we had been playing, and I was expecting him to talk about the rice seedlings that we had spoiled. Instead he stooped and scooped up a handful of mud. "What is this?" he asked.

The biggest boy among us took the responsibility of answering for us all. "It's mud, Tata."

"Whose mud is it?" the old man asked.

"It's your mud, Tata. This is your field."

Then the old man turned and looked at the nearest of the little channels across the dam. "What do you see there in that channel?" he asked.

"That is water, running over into the lower field," the biggest boy answered.

For the first time Tata looked angry. "Come with me and I will show you water."

We followed him a few steps along the dam, and he pointed to the next channel, where clear water was running. "That is what water looks like," he said. Then he led us back to our nearest channel, and said, "Is that water?"

We hung our heads. "No, Tata, that is mud, muddy water," the oldest boy answered. He had heard all this before and did not want to prolong the question-and-answer session, so he hurried on, "And the mud from your field is being carried away to the field below, and it will never come

9

back, because mud always runs downhill, never up again. We are sorry, Tata, and we will never do this again."

But Tata was not ready to stop his lesson as quickly as that, so he went on to tell us that just one handful of mud would grow enough rice for one meal for one person, and it would do it twice every year for years and years into the future. "That mud flowing over the dam has given my family food every year from long before I was born, and before my grandfather was born. It would have given my grandchildren food, and then given their grandchildren food forever. Now it will never feed us again. When you see mud in the channels of water, you know that life is flowing away from the mountains." [1]

Nilgiri Hills

Paul Brand then recounts how he returned to another similar area of South India, the Nilgiri Hills, thirty years later, in the 1950's. When he had visited it as a boy, the steep hills were thickly forested, the only cultivated plants allowed were tea, coffee or fruit trees, which were all good at holding the soil. The streams and rivers were clear and beautiful. But in the 1950's it was a different story. There was a new breed of landowner - people who had suffered in the great struggle for independence and had been rewarded with gifts of land. They knew nothing about the land. They never had a Tata to teach them the value of the soil. All they knew was that they wanted to make money and make it fast. The climate was ideal for growing potatoes and there was a market for them. So they cut down the trees and planted potatoes. They could harvest two or three crops a year and they soon got rich. But the land got poor. Potatoes don't hold the soil and the monsoon rains soon washed the earth away turning the streams to mud.

Thirty more years have passed and now Paul Brand says he doesn't enjoy going back to the Nilgiri Hills any more, although many parts of them are still beautiful. The slopes that were once covered with forests and then planted with potatoes are bare rock now. The streams that once ran crystal-clear and then flowed mud, today are dry.

Oh, Tata! Where have you gone? You have been replaced by businessmen and accountants who have degrees in commerce and who know how to manipulate tax laws, by farmers who know about pesticides and chemical fertilizers but who care nothing about leaving soil for their great-grandchildren. [2]

Of course, this kind of abuse of natural resources is not isolated to certain areas of South India. The same thing has happened and is continuing to happen all over the world. The tragic flooding in Bangladesh is caused by the same destruction of the forests in north India and Nepal. The famines in Ethiopia are directly attributable to, among other things, generations of destruction of the forests and neglect of the land because of injustices and abuses. Paul Brand comments:

11

There might not have been a famine today if the trees had not all been cut down, if the land had not eroded away, if the absentee landlords of Ethiopia had not been so greedy, and if the church had insisted that justice should prevail.[3]

Flowing farms

It is not only in developing countries that the problem of soil erosion exists. Paul Brand now lives beside the mighty Mississippi in Louisiana and can watch whole farms flow past his house every hour. Iowa has lost more than half of its topsoil in the century since people started farming there. Modern 'efficient' farming methods, encouraged by big-profit-seeking companies, involve an abandonment of traditional contour ploughing in favour of big machines ploughing straight up and down, which causes the soil to be lost at an even greater rate.

Deforestation and soil erosion are urgent matters. Paul Brand has dedicated his life to caring for people, to restoring the hands and feet of leprosy sufferers, but he says that he would gladly give up medicine and surgery tomorrow if by so doing he could have some influence on policy with regard to mud and soil.

The world will die from lack of soil and pure water long before it will die from lack of antibiotics or surgical skill and knowledge. But what can be done if the destroyers of our earth know what they are doing, and do it still? What can be done if people really believe that free enterprise has to mean an absolute lack of restraint on those who have no care for the future? [4]

I have chosen to begin by looking at the questions of deforestation and soil erosion raised by Paul Brand, because I believe they immediately show the importance of environmental or green issues. We may be unclear about the impact of global warming, pollution and nuclear power, but we all have to eat and we readily understand our dependence and the dependence of other living things on the soil. It is clear that we can, like the ancient king of Babylon, 'make the world a desert' (Isaiah 14:17), or like the Israelis at the present time, make the desert 'blossom as the rose' (Isaiah 35:1, AV).

Sutherland Hills

I too grew up amongst the hills, but very different hills from those of South India - the hills of Sutherland in the North-west Highlands of Scotland. The area has been called the last great wilderness in Europe. My father was a shepherd on a hill sheep farm near the north end of the Strath of Kildonan, the scene of some of the worst of the Highland Clearances, so from an early age I was aware of some of the issues affecting land use (and abuse) and the controversy surrounding it.

Towards the end of the eighteenth century and the beginning of the nineteenth century great efforts were made to 'improve' the Highlands. Following Culloden in 1746 and the attendant disintegration of the clan system, clan chiefs became even more isolated from the lives and needs of their people. It was apparent that there was growing poverty, but this was often put down to the idleness of the people instead of the neglect of the landowners.

The generally recommended 'improvement' for the Highlands was the removal of the people to the barren coasts or beyond to America, and their replacement with sheep. It is widely believed today that although the short-term suffering was regrettable, the landlords had really no alternative: the people faced starvation and poverty if they remained. But there was an alternative. This is clearly shown by the contrast between the proposals of Sir John Sinclair of Caithness and those which found favour on the neighbouring Sutherland estate.

Although Sinclair was a firm believer in improvement and in the virtue of sheep, his primary concern was for the welfare of the people.

> Nothing could be more detrimental than the mode now used of converting cattle into sheep farms in the Highlands. The first thing which is done is to drive away all the present inhabitants. The next is to introduce a shepherd and a few dogs and then to cover the mountains with flocks of wild, coarse-wooled and savage animals which seldom see their shepherd. The true plan of rendering the Highlands valuable would be to follow a different system. As many as possible of the present inhabitants ought to be retained. They ought to be gradually brought to exchange their cattle for a sufficient flock of valuable sheep.[5]

A somewhat different programme was implemented by the Duke of Sutherland (the English husband of the Countess of Sutherland). Although they were the richest noble family in Britain, they were less concerned with the wellbeing of their people than with the profitability of their estate. (Ironically, as it turned out, their 'improvements' were not a financial success.) Thousands were evicted from their ancestral homes to make way for sheep. In fact by 1811 around 15,000 tenants on the Sutherland estates had been moved to make way for an equal number of sheep. The attitude to the remaining people was shown by the report in that year by the factors of the Sutherland estate to the Board of Agriculture:

> Situations in various ways will be fixed on for the people. Fishing stations in which mechanics will be settled; inland villages, with carding machines; moors and detached spots calculated for the purpose will be found, but the people must work. The industrious will be encouraged and protected, but the slothful must remove or starve, as man was not born to be idle, but to gain his bread by the sweat of his brow. [6]

That last attempt to justify their injustice by biblical reference is rich coming from these irreligious hired men who did not even shrink from burning the homes of some of the most Christian people in the kingdom. But be that as it may, the promised 'inland villages' never materialised, and the 'moors and detached spots' are more desolate now than when they were first cleared. I could take you today to the isolated green patches and stoney mounds among the rolling hills, the tell-tale signs of pre-Clearance settlements - to Ascaig and Feranich and Aultanduin, or to Reiske from where my mother's people were evicted shortly after 1818.

In the later Nineteenth century sheep farming proved less profitable and following the romantic interest in the Highlands created by Queen Victoria, many estates were turned over to 'sport' - hunting, shooting and fishing. The two interests, sporting and sheep-farming, remained in uneasy partnership as the two main land uses in the North-West Highlands well into the middle of this century. One spin-off of this was the wholesale destruction of much wildlife - not so much the animals that were hunted, as their populations were generally carefully controlled, but the predators, the eagles, the buzzards, the peregrines, the foxes, the wild-cats, the badgers. In fact it is only in recent years as the estates have become run-down due to lack of funds, that the population of these animals has recovered.

Another spin-off was that sheep-farming came to be regarded as more peripheral to the main purpose of the estates which was to provide summer and autumn sport for absentee, mainly English landowners. I well remember some of the arguments my father had with factors concerning the need to cultivate and reclaim the land for agricultural use to make the sheep-farming more viable, so that ultimately more people could remain on the land. To some extent I believe he proved his case. But isolated experiments have not halted the continued depopulation of the Highlands. The wind sighs in quiet lament now not only over the tumbled ruins of the evicted, but also over many a shepherd's and gamekeeper's house. The absentee landlord has been one of the banes of the Highlands.

Wilderness or desert?

Other changes have come too since I was a boy in those hills. We lived on the very edge of what has become famous as 'the flow country' (pronounced by us locals to rhyme with 'allow' not 'blow'). It is one of the largest areas of blanket bog in western Europe. It has a unique range of wildlife including the Black Throated Diver, the Greenshank and the Golden Eagle. As such it has become an area of particular interest to ornithologists and conservationists. But also in recent years the Forestry Commission, private forestry companies and some landowners, keen to make use of otherwise unproductive land, planted sizable areas of this unique landscape with pine trees. Unfortunately, trees need no tree-herds, and although forestry will give long-term returns on investment and short-term employment, it will not significantly affect the depopulation of the Highlands.

And of course again we have a conflict of interests - this time between the conservationists and the foresters. Many conservationists argue that the present wilderness should be kept unchanged for its unique flora and fauna, and they deplore the destruction of the habitat of these marvellous species by the

17

drainage of the peat bogs and the wholesale plantation of lodgepole pine. The advocates of afforestation, however, point out that forestry is providing some kind of local industry which wildlife does not.

This conflict too raises interesting issues. Again, the way the land is being used is determined by a new breed of 'absentee landlords' who have little or no real contact or empathy with the local people. After all, human beings too are a threatened species in the Highlands, but there seems little concern for the continuing decline in the human population in the northern straths.

The idea of conservation is a problematic one also. The intention is usually to get back to some ideal 'natural' situation. But how far back do you go? If you go back far enough, you find that most of the north of Scotland was covered with forest. When we used to cut the peats, we often came across the remains of these old trees under the layer of peat. Equally, although forestation may destroy the habitat of some species, such as the divers and waders, it provides excellent habitat for harriers, owls, black grouse and many other species. So forestation is not all bad news in wildlife terms. However, there is no doubt that the wholesale planting of these northern peatlands would destroy a unique environment, which, once destroyed, would be almost impossible to replace.

Another ecological dilemma is posed by the presence of Dounreay, a nuclear power station on the northern edge of this 'last great wilderness of Europe' and a mere 25 miles from the hills where I grew up. To the anti-nuclear lobby its distinctive sphere is an intrusive blot on the landscape and its presence a mute threat to one of the most unspoiled areas of the world. But to many of the people living in that area it is a lifeline. Without it, far fewer of the young people of the neighbouring crofting communities would have been able to stay in the area. Dounreay has been a major provider of employment for Caithness and north Sutherland. So anyone recommending the closure of the nuclear plant, or even opposing its diversification into disposal of nuclear waste, must also recommend a viable scheme providing comparable employment, unless, of course, the idea is to completely empty the whole of that northern corner of Scotland of the indigenous Mackays, Sutherlands, Gunns, Murrays, Sinclairs and MacDonalds and turn it into a playground for City financiers and weekend environmentalists.

But it must be said that there are grave dangers in connection with Dounreay and not only in the possibility, however small, of nuclear pollution. There is the grave danger of any fragile human community becoming overdependent on one source of employment and wealth. This holds true not only for Dounreay, but also for the oil construction industry at Nigg and Kishorn and Ardersier. One day these yards, workshops and laboratories will be as derelict as the fish-curing sheds in Helmsdale, but the people and the hills, God willing, will still be there. So we see again that there are no easy or quick solutions to environmental and human dilemmas.

The solution is surely to find some sort of balance in man's management of the environment. The Highlands (and Highlanders) have suffered too long from wholesale measures imposed from outside by those with power and money. The answer does not lie in the wholesale replacing of trees with SSSIs (Sites of Special Scientific Interest) or the wholesale replacing of sheep with trees, any more than it lay in the wholesale replacing of people with sheep 170 years ago. Nor does the answer lie in large-scale industrial development only, unless that development engenders lasting small-scale business which can outlive the inevitable demise of short-term industries like oil. Unless there is some balanced management of the environment and industry of the North-west Highlands, the area may soon cease to be a wilderness and become a desert.

The problem is getting a balanced management. And you cannot get a balanced management unless you have a balanced philosophy - one that takes account of man's place and purpose in the environment as well as the place and purpose of animals. Our problem at the end of the twentieth century is that we have no basic agreement in the area of philosophy or cosmology. We have moved from the time when there was a Christian consensus. As we shall see, some regard that as no bad thing. They hold Christianity largely to blame for our ecological problems. But, be that as it may, we have now entered a time when there is no basic consensus.

There are competing ideas and interests in a pluralistic world. Of course, attempts are being made to replace Christianity with secular humanism, or more recently, with New Age thinking. It is the purpose of this book to show that neither secular humanism nor New Age provides the needed consensus to tackle the urgent ecological problems of the world. It is my conviction that we need to develop a Christian ecology. But before I can pursue my argument, we need to look at ecological problems on a world scale.

References

1. Paul W. Brand, 'A Handful of Mud: A Personal History of My Love for the Soil', in *Tending the Garden*, ed. Wesley Granberg-Michaelson, (Eerdmans, 1987), ps. 137-138
2. Granberg-Michaelson, *op. cit.*, p.140
3. Granberg-Michaelson, *op. cit.*, p.14
4. Granberg-Michaelson, *op. cit.*, p.147
5. Quoted in *Scotland's Story - A New Perspective*, Tom Steel, (Collins, 1984), p.218
6. Quoted in *Scotland's Story - A New Perspective*, Tom Steel, (Collins, 1984), p.218

CHAPTER 2

THE PRESENT CRISIS

Environmental problems are not new. Deforestation has been going on for thousands of years. The fertility of ancient Mesopotamia in Bible times was caused in large measure by the erosion of soil due to deforestation in the head-water regions of the Tigris and Euphrates rivers, and the deposition of this soil in the lower reaches. But this fertility was maintained only by a complex irrigation system which collapsed with the breakdown of effective political organisation in the region. Pollution too is an age-old problem.

> Water-borne diseases, like cholera, have been a fact of life in the Indian sub-continent for millenia . . . Symptoms of schistosomiasis (a disease which is perpetuated by faecal and urinary contamination of the water supply) have been recognised from descriptions on Babylonian inscriptions and Egyptian papyri 3,000 or more years old, and ova of the schistosome parasite have been recovered from mummies from the twentieth Dynasty (1200 BC).[1]

Environmental problems are not new, and awareness of environmental problems is not particularly new either. When I was a student in the late sixties, ecology was one of the 'in' ideas. But generally speaking such concerns were written off as alarmist, and in the seventies and most of the eighties the western world pressed on in its materialistic consumerism. All that has now changed. It is impossible to pick up a newspaper or magazine or watch an evening's television without noticing that some aspect of green issues is considered of vital importance. Environmental concerns are very firmly on the agendas of all the political parties.

How has this radical change come about? It is partly because of the success of those pressure groups formed in the sixties and early seventies like Greenpeace and Friends of the Earth. But it is also largely due to the fact that, in the public perception, green arguments have great plausibility at a common sense level. Before we proceed any further we must look at the specific issues which the Green Movement has brought to public attention.

Conservation of Resources

We have already noticed the importance of forests as a resource to prevent soil erosion. But of course trees are a resource in themselves in many different ways. In many areas of the underdeveloped world, trees are one of the main sources of fuel for heating and cooking purposes. And throughout the world wood is a common building material. These uses of trees involve the destruction of the trees and so it is vital that for every tree cut down, another tree is planted. Otherwise the resource will quickly be exhausted.

However, trees are also resources in ways that do not involve their destruction, but rather necessitate their continued life. Fruit trees are an obvious example. But all trees provide food and shelter for many species other than man, and so are a resource for life at many levels. Although tropical rainforests cover only 6% of the world's land surface, within them live more than half and perhaps as much as nine-tenths of all animal and plant species. This is largely an unused resource. Only a tiny proportion of species with potential value for food, medicine and other uses have so far been utilised.

Recently, yet another aspect of the importance of forests has been discovered. Tropical rain-forests especially, because of the density of their foliage, are responsible for the consumption of large amounts of CO_2. This is important not only for maintaining the right balance of oxygen in the air, but also for maintaining the 'Greenhouse Effect' at a constant level. This is an extremely complex subject, which we will consider in more detail when we look at global warming, but it is reasonably obvious that if we continue to destroy the rain-forests at the present rate, it is possible that the natural balance will be irrevocably altered.

It is estimated that the world's forests are disappearing at a rate of 15 million hectares a year - 11 million hectares in tropical regions. In Brazil an area of rainforest the size of Belgium is destroyed every year - all for the sake of producing more beef for the affluent nations of the world. 'It is therefore no exaggeration to say that every time a person bites into a hamburger, a chunk is taken out of the rainforest.'[2]

Another reason for the destruction of the rainforest is simply logging - the harvesting of hardwood for the timber industry of rich nations like Japan and the USA. Irish Columban missionary Sean McDonagh tells how the rainforest of the Philippines is being transformed into desert by the combination of uncontrolled logging by multinational companies and the local rich and by the desperate slash-and-burn cultivation techniques of the landless poor.[3]

The sea is a source of food resources which until quite recently was thought to be inexhaustible. This has proved not to be the case. Greedy exploitation has led to diminishing returns. The obvious example is whaling. In 1933 nearly 29,000 whales were caught yielding 2.6 million barrels of whale oil. By 1966 the figures were 58,000 whales, but only 1.5 million barrels. The reason was that larger species were hunted to extinction or near extinction and the industry turned to smaller and less productive species.

East-coast herring fishing in Britain is another example. To provide greater catches, fine-mesh nets were used. But fine-mesh nets caught immature fish as well as old. Few young fish were left to breed. The result was that the herring stock was destroyed by 1969.

There is a now well-known adage which says, 'Give a man a fish and you feed him for a day; teach a man to fish and you feed him for the rest of his life.' In the light of our recent discoveries concerning the depletion of resources this should now be revised to read, 'Give a man a fish and you feed him for a day; teach a man to fish and you feed him until the fish-stocks run out; teach a man to manage the fish resources and you feed him and his descendents after him for the rest of their lives.'

There are many other areas where the conservation of resources is important. These include mineral resources, oil, coal and gas; agricultural land and fresh water. However, as most of these involve questions of pollution we will now turn to that whole area.

Prevention of Pollution

As I indicated at the beginning of this chapter, pollution is not a new problem. Ever since human population was concentrated into cities there has been the problem of the disposal of human excrement. What could be safely and even beneficially disposed of when people were widely distributed in the country, became a health hazard in cities. It was not only in the ancient Middle East that this was a problem. Western cities were similarly afflicted until quite recent times. It was not until the stink of sewage from the Thames became intolerable in the Houses of Parliament that something was done about London's sewage system. (Therein lies a lesson for environmentalists and all lobbyists!)

Although the discharge of untreated sewage still causes problems in rivers and seas, industrial and agricultural pollutants are even more dangerous. Industrial pollution is not of recent origin. As far back as the Middle Ages (and no doubt earlier) people were complaining about the pollution caused in streams and rivers by metal-working. But it was the Industrial Revolution which gave rise to the large-scale pollution we have become familiar with. A Royal Commission Report in 1872 stated concerning Scottish rivers:

> ... the Dighty, Lothian Esk and Almond, the Gala and Kimarnock water, the Kelvin and the Cart are hardly equalled anywhere for filthiness; and the Clyde is beautiful or disgusting according as it is taken in the upper or lower reaches of its course. [4]

Scottish rivers have been cleaned up considerably in recent years. In 1983 salmon returned to the river Clyde after an absence of 120 years. But in some other areas of Europe, the Adriatic, the Rhine and especially Eastern Europe, the situation is extremely bad. Fish are either killed off altogether or else contain dangerously high levels of toxic metals like mercury. Similar problems exist right across the world from the Great Lakes in North America to Mindanao in the Philippines. For instance, in Japan factories discharged mercury-contaminated water into Minamata Bay over many years.

> At least 10,000 people who have eaten seafood from the area are now experiencing varying degrees of disability. Some are paralysed completely, others are suffering from varying degrees of blindness or chronic headaches.

Deaths from what is now known as the Minamata disease have already exceeded six hundred. [5]

Another problem caused by industrial processes is acid rain. The dangerous effects of gases released in coal-burning were known from early days in Britain. (Possibly that is why Edward I threatened torture and execution for the crime of burning coal!) It was not until the middle of this century, however, after the infamous London smog of 1952 which caused the death of 4000 people, mostly from respiratory disorders, that legislation was brought in. The long-term result of this has been to reduce the problems locally, but move them elsewhere. Less coal is burned domestically, but more is burned in power stations which release sulphur dioxide (SO_2) much higher into the atmosphere via their high chimneys. The SO_2 may then be carried for hundreds of miles before being deposited as dilute sulphuric acid which, of course, is very destructive to plant and fish life especially. In this way SO_2 produced in Britain affects Scandinavia and that produced in the USA affects Canada. Thousands of freshwater lakes in these areas are now so acidic that all life forms are dying. In Sweden 18,000 lakes out of a total of 96,000 are affected.

Oil too is not without its problems. Indeed, when pollution is mentioned most people think of oil. This is probably because when things go wrong in the oil industry they go spectacularly wrong and receive massive media exposure. Most of these incidents involve the shipwreck of oil tankers, from the *Torrey*

Canyon in 1967 to the *Amoco Cadiz* in 1978 to the more recent *Exxon Valdez*. But worse still was the deliberate sabotage of the Kuwaiti oil industry by the Iraqis during the Gulf War. Not only was there the destruction of sea life, but also the horrendous pollution of the atmosphere by the burning oilfields; all this in addition to the sheer waste of precious resources.

While the Industrial Revolution and its aftermath are linked to pollution in the minds of many people, fewer think of the effects of the agricultural revolution of the twentieth century. Changes in agricultural methods are also responsible for large-scale pollution of land, rivers and oceans. The main culprits are chemical fertilisers and pesticides. The best known pesticide with harmful long-term effects is DDT but there are many others. And even although use of DDT and other dangerous chemicals is now being severely restricted in the First World a great deal of damage continues to be done especially in Third World countries where agrochemical multinationals dump chemicals not permitted elsewhere. The problem with these toxic pesticides is twofold.

First, they are very long-lasting. Once they get into the soil, they can last for many years, or they can get washed down rivers and into the oceans. Such is the pollution of the sea that DDT has been found in the bodies of birds and fish in the Arctic. Secondly, they are not selective. They kill beneficial organisms like earthworms as well as pests.

Chemical fertilisers also cause pollution. One of the best known examples is the process known as eutrophication caused by nitrates being washed off land into rivers and lakes (Lake Erie, for example). This contributes to the rapid growth of large quantities of algae. When the algae die, the resulting decay consumes all the available oxygen in the water, causing the death of most other life-forms.

Global Warming and the Ozone Layer

Two areas of present concern in atmospheric pollution are the destruction of the ozone layer and global warming. These are two distinct problems although there is probably a good deal of confusion of the two in the popular mind. The ozone layer in the stratosphere protects the Earth from harmful ultraviolet radiation which can cause skin cancers and cataracts. It is now believed that gases called chlorofluorocarbons (CFCs), which are used in aerosol cans and refrigerators, destroy this high level ozone. In 1985 a hole was discovered in the ozone layer over Antarctica and many scientists believe there is considerable cause for concern. Although depletion of the ozone layer and global warming are distinct issues, yet there are two links. CFCs are also among the gases which are thought to contribute to global warming. But there is another more interesting link.

The chemical processes going on in the ozone layer depend on the temperature. Although this is a secondary effect, it is currently believed that any increased Greenhouse Effect will partially compensate for the destruction of ozone in the stratosphere. [6]

This illustrates how complex many ecological issues are. It is difficult to foresee the long-term effects of changes taking place today. In this regard there is probably no area more controversial than that of global warming.

There is a natural 'Greenhouse Effect' whereby the gases in the Earth's atmosphere act like the glass in a greenhouse keeping the Earth warm. If there was no atmosphere, a lot of the heat from the sun would be reflected back into space and the Earth would be too cold for most life-forms (average temperature minus 19^0C instead of the present 15^0C). It is thought by some scientists that the increase in the quantities of some gases like CO_2 and CFCs will cause more heat to be kept in the atmosphere and the earth's temperature will rise leading to melting of polar ice, rising oceans and flooding as well as increasing deserts.

What evidence is there for this rather alarming scenario? There seems to be little doubt that we have been increasing the amount of CO_2 and CFCs (referred to as trace gases) in the atmosphere. CO_2 is increased in two ways - the burning of fossil fuels and wood and the cutting down of forests and the resultant increase in desert. The former releases CO_2 directly into the atmosphere, while the latter decreases the amount of vegetation which converts CO_2 into oxygen. It is also generally agreed that the average global temperature increased by 0.5^0C between 1860 and 1980. However, there are various problems in making a direct correlation between these two developments.

> . . . the change in the greenhouse effect (in a strict sense) owing to changes in trace gas concentration, can be calculated with confidence, whereas prediction of the climatic change which may result is subject to considerable uncertainty, and the change may develop fully only after considerable delay. There are many factors other than trace gas concentrations which can affect climate. It has not yet been possible to identify changes in climate which can be attributed with certainty to changes in the greenhouse effect. [7]

In addition to this uncertainty there is the fact that the mid-nineteenth century marked the end of the so called 'Little Ice Age', a cold period lasting three hundred years, after which some increase in temperature might be expected. However, in spite of these reservations, many scientists believe that we cannot be too complacent. They believe it is better to be safe than sorry and recommend that we seek to reduce the emission of gases which tend to increase the greenhouse effect.

Nuclear Contamination

For most ordinary people the one thing that expresses best the concern over green issues is the threat of nuclear contamination. With the end of the Cold War and the consequent reduction in the threat of nuclear war, attention has turned to the nuclear power industry. This is especially so after the disastrous accident at Chernobyl in 1986. Only 31 people died immediately, but over 250 people died as a result in the following three years and thousands more are expected to die over the next twenty years from radiation-induced cancers. Agriculture was affected for years afterwards, not only in Russia but also thousands of miles away in Scotland.

Why is nuclear power so dangerous and why is it so desirable? The answer to both questions is the same. It provides massive power from a very small amount of fuel. Whereas most other forms of power generation involve a mere chemical reaction (hydrocarbon + oxygen = heat + CO_2 + H_2O), nuclear power is generated by the disintegration of an atom into two smaller atoms. This disintegration of the actual structure of a substance releases a huge amount of energy. A nuclear power station harnesses this power by a tremendously complex process. Unfortunately, the high power yield is only obtained by a process that is hazardous from beginning to end.

There is the danger of radioactivity from the original mined uranium right through to the highly radioactive waste products, some of which will remain radioactive for thousands of millions of years! The effects of radioactivity can range from immediate death to slow death caused by cancer to hereditary disease. Consequently, extreme safety measures are employed, but since Chernobyl scientists have not been quite so confident about these.

Preservation of nature
It is probably true that most of us can appreciate the common sense arguments in favour of conservation

of resources and prevention of pollution, because in these areas it is relatively easy to see the benefits for human beings. The disagreements will tend to be over questions of cost and scientific evidence. However, it is when we turn to the third area of green concern, preservation of nature, that disagreements can come at a more radical level. It is here that we tend to have a head-on clash between those who believe it is man's right to exploit nature as he sees fit and those who believe that nature should be preserved at all costs. This debate is fraught with many difficulties.

First there is the question of who is meant by 'man'. Is 'man' the land-hungry cattle ranchers on the fringes of the Amazonian rainforest, or is 'man' the Indian who inhabits the rainforest? Is he the Highlander living for generations on the land, or the wealthy landowner wishing to evict him? There can surely be no simplistic appeal to 'the rights of man'. Then there is the question as to what is the 'nature' that is to be preserved. Is it the present wilderness of the Highlands with its particular wildlife, or is it the tree-covered Highlands of the more remote past? Is it the present Sahara desert with its own peculiar flora and fauna, or is it the more lush landscape from which it has probably degenerated? If it is the latter that is in mind then it is not so much preservation that is wanted, but restoration with the consequent destruction of the present habitat of animals and birds.

However, having said that, I think most people would agree that the world would be a far poorer place without the great blue whale or the Siberian tiger or even the golden eagle. But of course that instinctive desire to preserve is based on our (human) sense of wonder and mystery at that which excites and moves us. It is not necessarily connected to any firm view about the value of a species in its own right or about how it fits into the complex interrelationships between species which exist in natural habitats.

Animal Rights

The debate becomes even more heated when we turn to the question of 'animal rights'. Incidentally, the term 'animal rights' is not a recent one. Eighteenth century farmer John Lawrence urged that 'the Rights of Beasts be formally acknowledged by the State'.[8] Utilitarian philosopher Jeremy Bentham spoke in similar terms. In the Christian tradition, John Wesley, William Wilberforce and Lord Shaftesbury all opposed cruelty to animals. However, it is in recent years that the issue of animal rights has come to prominence and usually in a more extreme form than previously. This is true not only of animal rights terrorists who will bomb those involved in animal experimentation, but also of serious moral philosophers like Peter Singer, who believes that 'speciesism' is just as wrong as racism or sexism. [9]

There are many vexed questions here. One is the question of blood-sports. Quite apart from whether it is right to take pleasure in killing, there still remain practical problems if blood-sports were banned. For instance, how would the red deer population of the Highlands be controlled if deer stalking ceased? Would we reintroduce the wolf? The fact is that the red deer has now no natural predators, and if the annual cull of stalking was discontinued, the numbers of deer would become far too great for the available grazing and thousands would die of starvation. Which death is more cruel for the deer: death by a bullet, death by a wolf's fangs or death by starvation?

Another problem is that posed by modern factory farming methods. There is no doubt that these methods have provided cheap food. But is economic value the only value? What about the value of animal life? What about the totally unnatural and horrible conditions in which many pigs and hens and calves are kept? The vast majority of egg-laying hens, for instance, are kept in cages measuring 20 inches by 18 inches with four or more hens in each cage! Mark Gold, Director of Animal Aid, has described many of these hens at the end of their service as having a combination of raw necks, deformed feet, tattered feathers, pale combs, abscesses and sores.[10] Even our very taste buds can tell the difference between a battery egg and a free range egg.

However, for many people it is not enough to insist upon good conditions for farm animals. They go further and argue either on principle or on practical grounds for some form of vegetarianism. In addition to the question of whether it is right for humans to eat animal flesh, there is also now the question of whether it is right for First World countries to import animal foodstuffs from the Third World thus reducing the amount of grain available to feed the starving. One third of all the grain produced in the world is fed to animals. Feeding grain to animals so that we can eat meat is a relatively inefficient method of using the nutritional value of grain. However, reducing the amount of meat we eat would not automatically feed the starving. Unless there are wide-ranging compensatory reforms, it could have a harmful effect on Third World economies.

Vivisection also raises important questions of animal rights. Is it right for us to operate on animals and test drugs on them, not for their own good but for our good? This not only poses the problem as to the relative value of human and animal life, but also raises questions as to what rights are and who gives rights. There is at present a move away from testing cosmetics and drugs on animals. Instead there is a move towards using human fetal tissue and perhaps even human fetuses instead. If testing such products on animals is deplorable, how can we justify the use of aborted human babies?

This confusion is further illustrated by the thinking of Peter Singer. On the basis of evolution he argues there is no clear dividing line between humans and animals. In addition, he reasons from the basis of utilitarianism ('the greatest happiness of the greatest number') that it is wrong to cause suffering for some animals. These are animals which seem closest to human beings, like whales, dolphins and apes, possibly monkeys, dogs, cats, pigs, seals and bears. He argues that they 'appear to be rational and self-conscious beings, conceiving themselves as distinct beings with a past and a future'. [11] If these animals are what he terms 'non-human persons', then it is just as wrong to hurt them or to kill them as it is to hurt or kill a human being. It may even be more wrong, if the human being in question is an infant or a mental defective.

Thus we see that this view, far from extending protection to all animals, actually reduces protection to cover only those organisms deemed by some human beings to qualify for protection. Ultimately, the question is: who decides which beings or organisms are capable of experiencing happiness or misery? We are left with relative human judgements. Today the chosen may include the higher animals; tomorrow unwanted humans may be excluded. Indeed, Singer specifically excludes unborn babies and newborn children up to one month old. 'Killing a defective infant is not morally equivalent to killing a person. Very often it is not wrong at all.'[12] Can you trust someone who holds such views to decide on animal rights? Frankly, I would not trust him with a rabbit.

In this, as in all the areas we have been discussing, we come up against the need for a consistent world view from which to tackle all these pressing problems. Throughout this century there has been a breakdown of the impact of a Christian world view on Western society with the result that we are now in a period of uncertainty. How long will this uncertainty continue? Will other world views, such as humanism or New Age thinking, take over from Christianity? Or will there be a rediscovery of a biblical Christian world view? These are questions that we cannot answer with certainty, but we can seek to answer the question as to what these world views have to offer in the area of ecology. This we will now seek to do.

References

1. Rowland Moss, *The Earth in Our Hands*, (IVP, 1982), p.14.

2. Tim Cooper, *Green Christianity*, (Spire, 1990), p. 27

3. Sean McDonagh, *To Care for the Earth*, (Geoffrey Chapman, 1986), p. 30ff

4. Quoted in *While the Earth Endures*, a report of the Science, Religion and Technology (SRT) Project of the Church of Scotland (1986), p. 57

5. Sean McDonagh, *To Care for the Earth*, (Geoffrey Chapman, 1986), p.22

6. Robert Harwood, 'The Greenhouse Threat', in *With Scorching Heat and Drought*? (SRT Project, 1989), p.7,8

7. Joe Farman, 'The Greenhouse Effect and Greenhouse Forcing of Climate', in *With Scorching Heat and Drought?*, (SRT Project, 1989), p.14

8. Quoted in Cooper, *op. cit.*, p. 227

9. Peter Singer, *Practical Ethics*, (Cambridge University Press, 1979), p. 48ff

10. See Cooper. *op. cit.*, p.232

11. Peter Singer, *op. cit.* p. 103

12. *ibid*, p. 138

PART 2

INTO A
SPIRITUAL
VACUUM

CHAPTER 3

WHOSE FAULT?

There seems to be little doubt in the minds of most scientific experts that we face an ecological crisis of considerable proportions. If that is so, before we can begin to put things right we must understand where we went wrong. For some it is sufficient to discover where our industrial and agricultural technologies have gone wrong in a strictly practical sense. But as we have seen, many of the areas of concern are controversial and people holding different world-views, starting with different assumptions, will come up with different conclusions. For instance, the way you treat animals will be determined by your view of what an animal is - a machine, a reincarnated soul or a fellow creature. Therefore, it is essential that we discover what worldview or complex of attitudes is responsible for the present crisis, before we seek to choose a worldview that we believe will solve our problems.

There appears to be a quite general consensus of opinion within the Green movement that orthodox Christianity is to blame for the ecological crisis. The argument may take a simple form or a more complex one. The simple argument says that the Bible teaches that man has dominion over creation. This is interpreted to mean that man can do as he pleases with the earth. This is the root of all the trouble. For instance, Max Nicholson, for many years Director-General of the Nature Conservancy, wrote:

> The first step must be plainly to reject and to scrub out the complacent image of Man the Conqueror of Nature, and of Man Licensed by God to conduct himself as the earth's worst pest.[1]

The more complex argument says that modern science and technology have caused the ecological crisis; Christianity gave birth to modern science; therefore Christianity is to blame. Of course, the more complex argument includes the simple one at the second stage of the argument. We will not look at this aspect in detail until we consider the Bible's teaching in Part 3.

Lynn White: Christianity to blame

The complex argument was first brought to general public attention in a now famous article by Lynn White in 1967. Lynn White was not an ecologist or even a scientist. He was professor of history at the University of California. The article, published in *Science Magazine*, was the text of a lecture delivered in 1966 and is entitled *The Historical Roots of our Ecologic Crisis*. Francis Schaeffer, who wrote *Pollution and the Death of Man* largely in answer to White's article calls it brilliant, and rightly so. Since it was a seminal piece of work that has had a profound influence on all subsequent thinking on ecology, I want to consider it in some detail. White first of all traces the beginnings of the present ecologic crisis to the combination of science and technology last century:

> . . . it was not until four generations ago that Western Europe and North America arranged a marriage between science and technology, a union of the theoretical and empirical approaches to our natural environment. The emergence in widespread practice of the Baconian creed that scientific progress means technological power over nature can scarcely be dated before 1850 . . . Its acceptance as a normal pattern of action may mark the greatest event in human history since the invention of agriculture, and perhaps in non-human terrestrial history as well. [2]

After demonstrating that science and technology both had their real beginnings in the Christian West in medieval times, he proceeds to examine Christian beliefs, because he believes that 'What people do about their ecology depends on what they think about themselves in relation to things around them. Human ecology is deeply conditioned by beliefs about our nature and destiny - that is, by religion.'[3] He sees the Christian doctrine of creation as central:

> Christianity inherited from Judaism not only a concept of time as non-repetitive and linear but also a striking story of creation . . . God planned

all this explicitly for man's benefit and rule: no item in the physical creation had any purpose save to serve man's purposes ... Especially in its Western form, Christianity is the most anthropocentric religion the world has seen ... Man shares in great measure God's transcendence of nature. Christianity, in absolute contrast to ancient paganism and Asia's religions ... not only established a dualism of man and nature but also insisted that it is God's will that man exploit nature for his proper ends.[4]

White next shows that this view of creation involves what has come to be known as 'desacralisation' - the destruction of the pagan recognition of spirits in the natural world. This is a thought that is developed in much more detail by other writers and is viewed by many as one of the deleterious effects of Christianity on ecology. He then proceeds to show why he believes that science arose under the influence of the Western form of Christianity and not the Eastern form.

Eastern theology has been intellectualist. Western theology has been voluntarist. The Greek saint contemplates; the Western saint acts. The implications of Christianity for the conquest of nature would emerge more easily in the Western atmosphere.'[5]

He points out that the early scientists from the thirteenth century up to Newton claimed to be 'thinking God's thoughts after him'. He concludes his analysis of the relationship between Christianity and science by saying:

> We would seem to be headed towards conclusions unpalatable to many Christians. Since both science and technology are blessed words in our contemporary vocabulary, some may be happy at the notions, first, that viewed historically, modern science is an extrapolation of natural theology and, second, that modern technology is at least partly to be explained as an Occidental, voluntarist realisation of the Christian dogma of man's transcendence of, and rightful mastery over, nature. But, as we now recognise, somewhat over a century ago science and technology - hitherto quite separate activities - joined to give mankind powers which, to judge by many of the ecologic effects, are out of control. If so, Christianity bears a huge burden of guilt. [6]

It is this implication of Christianity in the guilt of Western science for the ecological crisis which we must now examine. It is a claim that has been repeated many times since White delivered his momentous lecture.

Science and Christianity

It is interesting that earlier this century, when science was viewed as a fundamentally good thing, its beginnings were represented as a revolution against Christianity by men like Copernicus and Galileo.

Now that science is being blamed for the ecological crisis, its beginnings are represented as being firmly in the Christian tradition. It is difficult not to think that there is some bias at work here! The truth is that the real history is far more complex than the writings of historians.

There can be little doubt that science would not have arisen but for the influence of Christianity on Western Europe. In addition to the points made by White concerning the doctrines of creation and man's special position in creation, there is the sheer fact of the knowability and reliability of God in the Christian faith and the emphasis on God being a law-giver. C. S. Lewis, after quoting philosopher of science A. N. Whitehead in support, stated that science arose because of the Christian belief in God as law-giver:

> Men became scientific because they expected Law in Nature, and they expected Law in Nature because they believed in a Legislator. In most modern scientists this belief has died: it will be interesting to see how long their confidence in uniformity survives it. Two significant developments have already appeared - the hypothesis of a lawless subnature, and the surrender of the claim that science is true. We may be living nearer than we suppose to the end of the Scientific Age.[7]

This raises a most interesting question. If Christianity is being blamed for the ecological crisis, and Christianity gave birth to science, can science survive in the post-Christian world desired by many? It is not really a question of the survival of Christianity. It is a question of the survival of science. If the roots die, the branches will surely not take long to follow. If Christianity is marginalised away from the centres of learning and political power in society, the fruits of science which we all enjoy (not least those most vociferous in its condemnation), may soon wither and die. When belief in law and rationality and order in nature ceases, the scientific impetus may falter. We may not be forging ahead to ever greater discoveries. We may be on the threshold of a new dark age.

Greek influence

However, there is another whole side to this question of the relationship between Christianity and science which is rarely considered. Christianity had a huge impact on the birth of science, but it was not the only influence. To read some authors one might be forgiven for thinking that Christianity was the only world-view to influence the West. That, of course, was not the case. The other major influence has been Classical thought, especially Greek philosophy, with its emphasis on what man can discover by his unaided reason rather than depending on revelation from God. This influence was maintained well into the twentieth century with the classics forming the basis of education, including the education of those who went on to become scientists.

It should not surprise us that science not only derives much of its terminology from Latin and Greek, but several of its key ideas also. Atomic theory was not first propounded by modern physicists, but by

48

Leucippus and Democritus, Greeks of the fifth century BC. (It is ironic that atom means 'indivisible', but now it is known that whatever atoms are they not indivisible particles, but are made up of ever smaller particles - protons, neutrons, electrons, neutrinos etc. - which may not even be particles!) Similarly a theory of evolution was first taught by Anaximander well over two thousand years before Darwin. The point is not that the ancient Greeks anticipated modern scientific experimentation, but that nineteenth century scientists viewed the world through spectacles borrowed from the ancient Greeks.

But of course the Greek influence came in much earlier, especially through late medieval Catholic theologians like Thomas Aquinas in the thirteenth century, through the Renaissance and later through the Enlightenment; in other words during the whole period when science and technology were developing. Through Aquinas especially came the emphasis that there was a place for unaided human reason - unaided, that is, by revelation from God. He was greatly influenced by the Greek philosopher Aristotle as well as by Christian theology and so his thought has been characterised as being 'two storey' - the upper storey of 'grace' and the lower storey of 'nature'. The upper storey concerned knowledge which required the revelation of God; the lower storey concerned knowledge which could be attained by unaided human reason. It was therefore necessary that, besides the philosophical disciplines investigated by reason, there should be a sacred doctrine by way of revelation.[8] This distinction between reason and revelation had far-reaching consequences. It became a basic assumption of Western thought right through the Renaissance and Enlightenment to the present day.[9]

Aquinas (and others such as William of Occam) opened the door to the influence of Greek philosophy on the West and helped to make man autonomous (a law to himself) in some areas, particularly in the area of man's relationship to nature. However, to begin with, the reintroduction of Greek thinking into Western thought caused a hostile reaction to science. This is clearly seen in the Roman Catholic Church's rejection of Copernicus and Galileo. Francis Schaeffer writes:

> When the Roman Church attacked Copernicus and Galileo it was not because their teaching actually contained anything contrary to the Bible. The Church authorities thought it did, but that was because Aristotelian elements had become part of church orthodoxy, and Galileo's notions clearly conflicted with them. In fact, Galileo defended the compatibility of Copernicus and the Bible, and this is one of the factors which brought about his trial. [10]

Renaissance and Reformation

Although there was a great impetus given to the influence of Greek thought in the period in the fourteenth, fifteenth and sixteenth centuries known as the Renaissance, there was a tremendous reaction to Greek influence in the sixteenth century Reformation. The crucial difference between the Renaissance and the Reformation was that, although they both reacted to the traditions of the Church, the Renaissance reacted even more in the direction of man-centred thinking, while the Reformation reacted in the direction of God-centred thinking.

While the central emphasis by Calvin and Luther was undoubtedly on man's relationship with God, even that emphasis was not expressed as man's ascent to God, but rather (in terms of what they found in the Bible) as God's descent to man. And, as Paul Santmire has pointed out in his meticulous study *The Travail of Nature*, they also had what he calls 'circumferential elements in their thought: the divine and human engagement with nature'. [11] Because nature was created by God the Reformers considered it important in its own right and not just as useful to man.

Calvin especially was not afraid to refer to the writings of the ancient Greeks or to the discoveries of science, because he believed 'All truth is from God ... Besides, all things are of God; and, therefore, why should it not be lawful to dedicate to his glory everything that can be properly employed for such a purpose?'[12] Calvin did not see life divided into two realms or two storeys of reason and revelation or nature and grace. He saw all life under the sovereign control of the Creator and all true knowledge whether scientific or religious as revealed by God, either in the book of God's works (nature) or the book of God's words (the Bible).

He shows that science is reading God's thoughts:

51

We are surrounded on every hand by proofs of the Creator's wonderful wisdom. Some of these are hidden from ordinary observation, and can only be brought to light by astronomy and other sciences ... Men who possess scientific knowledge can penetrate more deeply into some of the secrets of divine wisdom ... It is true that exact and scientific observation is required if we are to investigate the motion of the heavenly bodies, to determine their orbits, to measure their distances, and observe their properties ... [13]

He rejects outright the idea, popular then as now, that attributes the beauty and order and design of the created universe, not to God but to nature itself or to 'some shadowy Power':

It is better to say that nature is an order which God has established. In matters of such importance, it is a mischievous mistake to confound God with the works which he has made, and with that course of nature which is subject to his will.[14]

Therefore nature is neither an alien world inhabited by gods and spirits, nor is it independent of God and subject purely to man's sinful desires. It is the realm of God's activity and revelation. It is not to be degraded, but it is to be reverently investigated, used and admired, for in it the glory of God is seen.

Early scientists like Galileo and Isaac Newton and Robert Boyle shared a similar view to that of Calvin concerning the relationship between religion and science, revelation and nature. Galileo said, 'Holy Scripture and nature equally proceed from the divine Word, the first as dictated by the Holy Spirit, the second as the very faithful executor of God's commands.' [15]

But while these men generally worked and wrote within a worldview that was God-centred, there is an ambiguity in certain of their statements such as the well-known words of Francis Bacon written in 1620:

> Man by the Fall fell at the same time from his state of innocence and from his dominion over creation. Both of these losses, however, can even in this life be in some parts repaired; the former by religion and faith, the latter by the arts and sciences. [16]

There is probably little doubt that Francis Schaeffer is right in his view that Bacon 'did not see science as autonomous, for it was placed within the revelation of the Scriptures at the point of the Fall'. [17] However, there is a measure of ambiguity in the separation of 'religion and faith' on the one hand from 'arts and sciences' on the other. The trend which culminated in the Enlightenment of the 18th century exploited this kind of ambiguity to the full.

Enlightenment

A change took place in Western thought which radically affected every area of life including science and theology. A pivotal role was played in this change by the German philosopher, Immanuel Kant. Paul

Santmire includes Kant's thought along with the natural sciences and 'the socio-political world of modern industrialism' as the major influences which came to alter the Reformation perception of nature:

> Something happened to the Reformers' thought about nature as the Reformation tradition unfolded. The tradition was decisively impacted to begin with, by three external cultural forces, each one intimately related to the others: first, from the side of the natural sciences; second ... the philosophy of Immanuel Kant; third, from the context of the socio-political world of modern industrialism. With their vision of reality influenced by these trends, many nineteenth and twentieth-century Protestant thinkers came to view nature no longer as a theatre of God's glory and power, in which humanity is essentially embodied, as it was for the Reformers. [18]

In answer to the question 'What is enlightenment?' Kant wrote:

> Enlightenment is man's release from his self-incurred tutelage. Tutelage is man's inability to make use of his understanding without direction from another... 'Have courage to use your own reason!' - that is the motto of enlightenment. [19]

The effect of Kant's views on religion was to replace revelation with reason - man's reason. His book on the subject was entitled *Religion within the Limits of Reason Alone*. He also made a division in knowledge between the noumenal world (the world of ethics and religion) and the phenomenal world (the world of science). He effectively separated God and nature. This separation has proved fateful for the modern world. Man is now left in splendid superiority over nature with no interfering God who speaks. Santmire rightly calls Kant's philosophy 'an ecological sieve'.[20] It effectively removed the Reformers' emphasis on the kingdom of God including nature.

So I believe Lynn White was wrong to lay the blame for the ecological crisis at the door of Christianity. To do so is like blaming Christianity and Judaism for the excesses of Communism because it can be shown that Communism is a Judeo-Christian heresy. Science and technology undoubtedly have their roots in Christianity, but Christianity is not anthropocentric, it is theocentric. The anthropocentric emphasis came from the Greeks, from the Renaissance and the Enlightenment.

To reject Christianity and to go back to pagan thought is to go back to the very roots that caused the problem in the first place - man's confidence in his own unaided reason to solve the problems. Such a return will also lead to the death of science, for it was Christianity that gave it birth, and it is clear that where a misdirected science has caused the ecological crisis, a redirected science will be required to provide a remedy. The question is: what worldview should redirect science? And if the world-view is not Christianity, can science itself survive in order to solve the problem?

References

1. Quoted by Rowland Moss in *The Earth in our Hands*, (IVP, 1982), p.9

2. Lynn White, 'The Historical Roots of our Ecologic Crisis', *Science Magazine*, March 10, 1967, reproduced in full by Francis Schaeffer in *Pollution and the Death of Man*, (Hodder and Stoughton, 1970), p. 72

3. *ibid.* ps. 77,78

4. *ibid. ps.* 78,79

5. *ibid. p.* 80

6. *ibid. p.* 82

7. C S Lewis, *Miracles*, (Fontana, 1960), p. 110

8. Thomas Aquinas, *Summa Theologiae*, 1, Question 1

9. See the writings of Francis Schaeffer especially *Escape from Reason* (recently republished by IVP as part of *Francis A Schaeffer Trilogy*) and *How Should We Then Live?*

10. Francis Schaeffer, *How Should We Then Live?*, (Fleming H Revell, 1976), p. 131

11. Paul Santmire, *The Travail of Nature*, (Fortress Press, 1985), p. 128

12. John Calvin, Commentary on Titus 1.12 in *Calvin's Commentaries*, (Delaware, AP&A), p. 2274

13. John Calvin, *The Institutes of the Christian Religion*, I.iv

14. *ibid.* I.iv

15. Quoted by Colin Brown, *Christianity and Western Thought*, (Apollos, 1990), p. 176

16. Quoted by Francis Schaeffer, *op.cit.*, ps. 134,135

17. Francis Schaeffer, *Escape from Reason*, in *Francis A Schaeffer Trilogy*, p. 226

18. Santmire, *op. cit.*, p. 133

19. Quoted by Colin Brown, *op. cit.*, ps. 285,286

20. Santmire, *op. cit.*, p. 135

CHAPTER 4

MATERIALIST MAGICIANS

An attractive calendar for 1991 was distributed in schools in the North-east of Scotland. It is entitled *Trees for Life* and it has superb photographs of a variety of trees from many parts of the world. It contains an article entitled 'From Germ to Giant' about the world's largest tree, the Giant Sequoia, and there is information about 'Regenerating the Caledonian Forest'. A casual glance would perhaps convince you that this was something produced by some purely environmental pressure group or even the Forestry Commission. In fact it is published by the Findhorn Foundation, a New Age community of worldwide reputation, based at Findhorn in Moray.

Alongside worthy ecological advice in the calendar, there are more esoteric and religious emphases:

... love is the essence of all life, and as humans, we have a unique opportunity to bring love to the world. At this time of increasing concern for the environment, we each have the power in our hearts to help in the healing of the Earth.'

Then there is this 'meditation' for the month of September:

> Even the smallest woods have their secrets and secret places, their marked precincts. And I am certain all sacred buildings from the greatest cathedral to the smallest chapel, and in all religions, derive from the natural aura of certain woodland or forest settings, in them we stand among older, larger and infinitely other beings, remoter from us than the most bizarre other non-human forms of life: blind, immobile, waiting . . . altogether like the only form a universal god could conceivably take. [1]

Because of examples like this, New Age thinking is linked to Green concerns in the minds of many. It is widely recognised that there is some connection. Clifford Longley writing in *The Times* said:

> The New Age is undoubtedly Green. It shares the contemporary perception of Planet Earth as a small and fragile globe which is mankind's one precarious home in the entire universe. The concept of Gaia, invented by Professor James Lovelock to describe the unity, the interdependence and the equilibrium of the planetary eco-system, offers New Ageism the beginnings of a theology, once Gaia is made to sound . . . like a mother goddess who is divine protectress of all living things. [2]

There is obviously some sort of relationship or interaction between New Age thinking and Green thinking. Is New Age the new philosophy that the world needs to deal with the ecological crisis? Or will it lead us down a blind alley?

New Age

What is New Age? And why is it becoming influential in thinking on Green issues? New Age thinking is notoriously difficult to define. This is because it has been formed by many different influences, ranging from astrology to astronomy, from eastern religion to modern theology, from positive thinking to spiritism. It is eclectic. It will draw from any source. Its name may come from astrology, but as we will see, it also claims to draw support from quantum physics and ecology.

The name 'New Age' comes from the belief in astrology that the history of the world is divided into ages corresponding to the signs of the zodiac. In the late Sixties the group The Fifth Dimension and the musical *Hair* announced the dawning of the Age of Aquarius. Marilyn Ferguson, in her influential book *The Aquarian Conspiracy* presents the view that approximately every 2000 years there is an astronomical shift of the vernal equinox to a new constellation of the zodiac. [3] She believes that at the turn of the century we will move from the Age of Pisces (the age of Christianity) into the Age of Aquarius (the age of peace, love and enlightenment). One of the reasons Pisces (the Fishes) is identified with Christianity is that early Christians chose the fish as a symbol. However, this was for a reason totally unrelated to astrology. The initial letters of 'Jesus Christ, God's Son, Saviour' in Greek make up *ichthus*, the Greek word for fish. But it is typical of New Age thinking that such interconnections are made. What to the rational mind is merely a coincidence is invested with deep significance by New Agers. Be that as it may, the New Age belief is that around the year 2000 we will pass into a New Age.

If Christianity is not going to be the predominant view of this New Age, what is going to be? According to New Agers it will be New Age thinking or 'the new consciousness'. New Age thinking hates distinctions or opposites. It loves 'inter-connectedness'. Instead of believing that God is distinct from human beings and human beings from nature, they believe that 'all is one'. Human beings are just part of nature and God is just a force or power in nature. Remember 'The Force be with you' in *Star Wars*? Well, 'The Force' was very much the New Age idea of God. It was a power that could be tapped by people and it had a 'dark side' or evil side which was used by the Emperor to ensnare Darth Vader. This idea that good and evil are all part of the One also appears at the end of the film *The Dark Crystal* where the good beings and evil beings are merged. What was wrong was that they had been separated.

There is one underlying belief in all New Age thinking and that is what has come to be known as pantheistic monism, the belief that all is one. God and the cosmos, man and nature, matter and energy are all one. So we see three things about the New Age idea of God that are completely different from the God who speaks in the Bible. New Agers believe God is not a Person but a power, not distinct from nature but within it, not absolutely good but a mixture of good and evil. In this New Age is not new! C. S. Lewis held that pantheism is the natural religion of fallen man:

> Pantheism is congenial to our minds not because it is the final stage in a slow process of enlightenment, but because it is almost as old as we are . . . It is immemorial in India. The Greeks rose above it only at their peak, in the thought of Plato and Aristotle; their successors lapsed into the great Pantheistic system of the Stoics. Modern Europe escaped it only while she remained predominantly Christian; with Giordano Bruno and Spinoza it returned. With Hegel it became almost the agreed philosophy of highly educated people, while the more popular Pantheism of Wordsworth, Carlyle and Emerson conveyed the same doctrine to those on a slightly lower cultural level. So far from being the final religious refinement, Pantheism is in fact the permanent natural bent of the human mind . . . It is the attitude into which the human mind automatically falls when left to itself. [4]

Pantheism was the underlying philosophy of the Stoics whom Paul met in Athens (Acts 17). For centuries it has been the unifying belief in Hinduism and Buddhism. In another of his perceptive comments, C. S. Lewis said that ultimately Hinduism and

Christianity would offer the only real alternatives, because Hinduism absorbs all religious systems and Christianity excludes all others. We see his prophecy being fulfilled in the New Age movement.

But where do human beings fit into the New Age scheme of things? This is where New Age differs from Eastern religion. In the East, Atman is Brahman (atman = the individual soul, brahman = the Absolute or 'God'). Every individual soul is a manifestation of the impersonal 'God', and salvation consists of the soul being absorbed back into 'God'. This loss of individuality in the East has never appealed to the Western mind. So what New Age thinkers have done is to turn the Eastern idea on its head and combine it with their version of Christian ideas. They say Brahman is Atman. It is the individual human soul that is important.

The actress Shirley MacLaine, a well-known New Age writer, takes the biblical words 'I am that I am', words that apply to God alone, and applies them to herself.[5] Now this is tremendously appealing in a West that does not want to give up its humanism, its emphasis on the individual human being. (By contrast the Christian humanism of the Apostle Paul is expressed in the words 'by the grace of God I am what I am' - 1 Corinthians 15:10) MacLaine goes even further. She believes she creates her own reality, including life and death and even God. It hardly needs to be said that this is even more attractive to our self-centred fallen human nature. It is the original temptation in the Garden of Eden - 'you will be like God' (Genesis 3:5).

So if human beings are divine and we are all part of one process, what's wrong with the world? And what has to be done to put it right? New Ageism does not believe in sin or guilt. It's not sin that's wrong with the world, but ignorance, what has been called 'metaphysical amnesia'. We have forgotten that we are God! They say this is because of 'straight-thinking' and Christianity. What we need is a 'paradigm shift' in thinking, the adoption of 'cosmic consciousness', that is to say, the awareness that we are the cosmos (the universe) and the cosmos is 'God'. Various things are recommended as useful to this end, ranging from eastern-style meditation through the use of crystals and pyramids to 'channelling' (spiritism) and other occult practices. Again, it is much easier for us to accept that we lack knowledge than that we lack righteousness; that we don't need to have our guilt removed, only our minds enlightened.

Another thing that people find attractive about New Age is that it is optimistic about the future. The twentieth century has been very pessimistic. There has been fear of nuclear war, fear of the unknown in the universe and fear of the unknown in death. But the New Age holds out hope - hope of there being 'One World' without wars and strife, hope of the end of the ecological crisis, man being at one with nature, hope of a life beyond death of your own choosing.

This last area is one where New Age thought has taken over something from Eastern religion and changed it. The Eastern idea of reincarnation is that after death you come back as someone (or even something) else according to a strict law of 'karma' -

a system of rewards and punishments based on your behaviour in your previous life. New Age has taken the idea of reincarnation but holds that a person simply chooses his new life. Now the Eastern idea at least retained some idea of morality even although it weakens the desire to help our fellow man. According to it, a poor sick man is being punished in this life for the sins of past lives. But the New Age idea is even worse. It says that the man has chosen his condition for his own spiritual development. So there is even less reason to help him.

But why is it that New Age thinking is coming to prominence in the area of ecology? What has happened to Christianity or even secular humanism? The fact is there is a spiritual vacuum at present. Christianity has been rejected, but secular humanism has never satisfied the soul of man, and both are deemed by many ecologists to be far too anthropocentric. There has, of course, been a rejection of Christianity in society at large, but particularly relevant here is the rejection of orthodox Christianity as an acceptable cosmology in relation to ecological issues (which we examined in the last chapter). Although Lynn White did not reject Christianity totally, yet he considered alternatives, such as the Zen Buddhism of the hippies, and he opened the door for others with a more radical approach.

The New Physics

Another factor that has played a part in opening the door to New Age thinking is the revolution that has taken place in science, especially in nuclear physics.

The distinction between matter and energy is broken down - $E=mc^2$ (where E=energy, m=mass and c=the speed of light) and atomic particles are now wave-particle dualities. Einstein's Theory of Relativity teaches that time and space are not absolutes, but variables that depend upon the position and the viewpoint of the observer, as well as the speed at which the observer is moving. Heisenberg's Uncertainty Principle says that we can determine the position or speed of a particle, but not both at the same time. There is also the possibility in quantum physics that the act of observing affects whether we judge something is a particle or a wave and what its position is. Bell's Theorem tells us that once two particles interact, anything that affects the direction of spin of one of the particles affects the direction of spin of the other particle, even if they are at opposite ends of the galaxy! It appears that something other than normal 'cause and effect' is operating, but nobody yet knows what it is.

All of this is used by New Agers as proof that the old certainties are breaking down and that there is a growing recognition of an inter-connectedness between everything in the universe. New Age physicist Fritjof Capra writes:

> Quantum theory has shown that subatomic particles are not isolated grains of matter but are probability patterns, interconnections in an inseparable cosmic web that includes the human observer and her consciousness. Relativity theory has made the cosmic web come alive. [6]

Shirley MacLaine puts it more popularly:

> As the new physics and the ancient mystics now seemed to agree - when one observes the world and the beings within it, one sees that we are in fact only dancing with our own consciousness'.[7]

C. S. Lewis predicted this contemporary combination of science and superstition. In *The Screwtape Letters*, the imaginary correspondence of a senior to a junior devil, he shows that one of the greatest triumphs of Satan will be to produce 'the Materialist Magician':

> If once we can produce our perfect work - the Materialist Magician, the man, not using, but veritably worshipping, what he vaguely calls 'forces' while denying the existence of 'spirits' - then the end of the war will be in sight. [8]

Gaia - Goddess of the Earth

One of the key concepts in the influence of New Age ideas in ecology has been the Gaia Hypothesis formulated by British scientist James Lovelock. According to Lovelock, the Earth itself may be seen as a self-regulating, living organism, which he called Gaia after the ancient Greek goddess of the Earth. He expresses it like this:

> The entire range of living matter on earth from whales to viruses and from oaks to algae could be regarded as constituting a single living en-

tity, capable of manipulating the earth's atmosphere to suit its overall needs and endowed with facilities and powers far beyond those of its constituent parts. [9]

He makes clear, however, that Gaia is not composed only of living things. It is the whole planet:

The name of the living planet, Gaia, is not a synonym for the biosphere. The biosphere is defined as that part of the Earth where living things normally exist. Still less is Gaia the same as the biota, which is simply the collection of all individual living organisms. The biota and the biosphere taken together form part but not all of Gaia . . . The Gaia Hypothesis, when we introduced it in the 1970s, supposed that the atmosphere, the oceans, the climate, and the crust of the Earth are regulated at a state comfortable for life because of the behaviour of living organisms . . . Life and its environment are so closely coupled that evolution concerns Gaia, not the organisms or the environment taken separately. [10]

To begin with, Lovelock presented Gaia as a purely scientific hypothesis, but in the last chapter of *The Ages of Gaia* entitled 'God and Gaia' he addresses the religious implications of the hypothesis.

I have tried to show that God and Gaia, theology and science, even physics and biology are not separate but a single way of thought. [11]

He became a member of Lindisfarne, a sort of New Age think-tank, who describe themselves as 'Seeking for the sacred in all forms of human activity and culture ... the spiritual transformation of individual consciousness ... the resacralisation of the relations between nature and culture ...' [12]

This blending of ecology and religion is typical of the New Age movement and of a school of thought in ecology known as 'Deep Ecology', but it is also common at the popular level. Richard North, environment correspondent of *The Independent* said:

An awful lot of us just need to worship something . . . We are all falling in love with the environment as an extension to and in lieu of having fallen out of love with God. As it happens it makes for a pretty deficient religion, but as an object of worship, nature takes some beating. [13]

Jonathan Porritt, a director of Friends of the Earth, has a high regard for New Age thinking and Buddhism:

All that one can incontrovertibly claim is that many thousands in the UK have found in New Age thinking and teaching a sense of hope and meaning that has eluded them elsewhere.

Only Buddhism can make any real claim to be permeated through and through with ecological awareness and guidance about 'right livelihood'. [14]

He also quotes with approval John Stewart Collis, whom he calls 'a visionary of the Green movement' as follows:

This is now regarded as a very irreligious age. But perhaps it only means that the mind is moving from one state to another. The next stage is not a belief in many gods. It is not a belief in one God. It is not a belief at all - not a conception in the intellect. It is an extension of the consciousness so that we may feel God, or, if you will, an experience of harmony, an intonation of the divine which will link us again with animism, the experience of unity lost and the in-break of self-consciousness. [15]

G. K. Chesterton put it more bluntly, but more accurately - 'When men cease to believe in God, they do not believe in nothing; they believe in everything.'

The Findhorn Faith

The Green aspect of New Age is shown especially by the Findhorn Foundation. David Spangler, a representative thinker of Findhorn, writes:

The Myth of Findhorn is the Myth of Creation, of a rebirth of man emerging into a totally new consciousness. The myth is not a few individuals gaining a higher understanding of the spiritual and cosmic principles behind life and creation, but a period when the planet as one shall begin to strip away the old personality patterns . . . and in its place reveal the true divine nature of the planet. [16]

In 1963, Dorothy Maclean, one of the leaders of Findhorn, claimed she started receiving messages from spirits (called Devas) which said that 'man has to do one thing in order to reverse the trend of events on the planet: he has to recognise within himself the divinity and wholeness of which he is part.' [17]

Sir George Trevelyan, who taught Prince Philip at Gordonstoun, is a prominent New Ager who supports both the Gaia Hypothesis and the Findhorn Community. In 1971 he founded the Wrekin Trust, an interdenominational organisation dedicated to teaching the spiritual nature of humanity and the holistic view of the universe. He says, 'We must learn to think wholeness, to realise the reality of the Earth mother and that our exploitation of the animal kingdom and the rest of nature is piling up for us an enormous karmic debt.' [18] This is a perfect example of the syncretism of New Age thinking. The Eastern concept of karma (judgement and fate) is linked with holistic thinking, the Gaia Hypothesis and ecological concerns.

The New Story

New Age thinkers are not alone in presenting some kind of religious response to the ecological crisis. The Irish Columban priest, Sean McDonagh, is one of those who sees the answer in the adoption of a new theology. This theology is based not primarily on the Bible as God's Word but on an evolutionary worldview as propounded by Teilhard de Chardin, the French Jesuit palaeontologist. He calls it 'the new story'.

The story of the universe, or cosmogenesis, as Teilhard calls it, has a double thrust - increased 'complexification' and expanded consciousness. We return to a familiar theme of the story. Any mechanistic approach to the universe, which merely articulates the physical dimension, is radically defective and dangerous when it becomes the basis of human activity.

The Cosmos is, in fact, a geophysical and biospiritual reality to which human beings must learn to relate in its totality... Carried along by this stream of thought, human beings reach their full stature in relation to the entire cosmic process ...

This affinity of being for being is a property of all life, as Teilhard stresses. If there were no pressure for simple molecules to unite, 'it would be impossible for love to appear higher up with us, in hominized form'. Love is the highest expression of this communion. It embraces the natural world, fellow human beings and ultimately God. [19]

71

McDonagh's position, and that of Teilhard which underlies it, is really offering a Christianised form of pantheistic monism. Santmire comments that, 'Teilhard feels compelled to postulate a primitive state of consciousness in all material things'.[20] In addition, Teilhard sees the physical universe as ultimately collapsing and disappearing, but that portion of the universe which had become self-conscious (humans) being finally merged with God. Although he sees nature as good, it is only good because it produces spirit, not because it is good in itself. This attitude comes out strikingly in his view of the sexual relationship of men and women. Although he views both the masculine and the feminine as good, he believes that the best relation between the sexes is the one that is not consummated. Although Teilhard's thought is self-consciously modern, here we are back to another form of Aquinas' two storey approach. Matter is only important as a vehicle for the spiritual. And the predominant motif in his thinking concerning the relation of humans to nature is conquest. As Santmire points out, this is hardly a helpful worldview in the present ecological situation.[21]

New Age - the Answer?

So how should we respond to New Age? Are we indeed entering a new age? There is no doubt that the world at the end of the twentieth century is very different from the world at the beginning of this century. There are of course all the obvious differences - means of travel, communication and warfare, all the developments of science, technology and medicine. But there are even greater changes in the way people think. And these have taken place much more recently amongst the general public. Although many of these ideas that we now call New Age were around in the Sixties, it was mainly among 'way out' people like rock musicians and hippies. Now these ideas are everywhere. No doubt a major factor in this is that those who were students in the Sixties are now in influential positions in the media, politics and industry. There has been a reaction against hard science and now people are much more prepared to accept 'spiritual' ideas ranging from astrology to alternative medicine to witchcraft.

However, not all in the environmental movement are happy with this development. We must be careful not to make the mistake of thinking that all that is Green is New Age. There are those, such as Murray Bookchin, who advocate 'Social Ecology' - really socialist and naturalistic ecology. According to this view there is no supernatural, and ecological problems are not caused by individual attitudes, but by a social order based on free-market, expansionary capitalism.

There is a running battle at the moment among environmentalists on the Deep Ecology/Social Ecology issue. But it appears to me that the greatest challenge to Christianity in this area will come from the Deep Ecology/New Age end of the environmental spectrum. The collapse of the Soviet Union has shown that a consistent naturalistic, socialistic, centralised policy is a failure, not least in environmental/pollution issues. People seem to be dissatisfied with a mechanistic, materialistic, rationalistic view of life and are turning in increasing numbers to worldviews that have some kind of religious dimension.

C. S. Lewis once made a fascinating prediction of the dawning of a new age. He was a great friend of J. R. R. Tolkien, the author of *The Hobbit* and *The Lord of the Rings* and he said of the latter book, 'Wouldn't it be wonderful if it really succeeded (in selling I mean). It would inaugurate a new age.' [22] Now, of course he did not mean by a new age what is now called New Age. Nevertheless his words set me thinking.

The Lord of the Rings is probably unique in that it has consistently increased its sales every year since it was published. Both Tolkien's and Lewis's writings are enjoying immense popularity among young people, although most are probably unaware of their Christian connotations. However, there is absolutely no doubt that people are far more open to the possibility of 'other worlds' than they were thirty years ago. Whether the writings of Tolkien and Lewis have created that openness or merely fed it, is not of primary importance. The fact of the openness is indisputable. Fantasy and mythology are big sellers in books, videos, board and computer games.

There is no doubt that this can be a dangerous thing. People may get led into the real world of the occult. But is this any more dangerous than the belief that science has explained everything and there is no room for God? I think not. Young people especially are turning away from the idea that the universe is one big machine and they are rediscovering a sense of mystery.

People are disillusioned with materialism, but they will be equally disappointed with New Age thinking. New Age has no sufficient answer in the area of ecology either. If, according to Shirley MacLaine, I am God and I think the cosmos into existence, then the reality, and therefore the importance, of the cosmos is lost. There cannot even be agreement that nature has an objective existence, because there is no guarantee that each person is thinking the same universe into existence. We are up against the same problem as in Eastern thinking - the world is *maya* (illusion).

Also, if all is one and all is God, then we have two problems. First, there is no basis for holding that human beings are distinguished from nature and in any way superior to nature. If that is so, then man has no right to interfere in nature even for supposedly 'good' reasons. In fact, second, there is ultimately no basis for distinguishing between good and evil at all, between cruel and non-cruel. If all is one and all is divine, how can we say some things are evil and to be fought against and some things are good and to be fought for? And if we cannot do that, how can we propose Green policies? We are again left with the fatalism of India where there is no impetus to change for the better from within Hinduism itself.

As far as 'the new story' of Teilhard and McDonagh is concerned, it does not provide the answers we need whether it is conceived of as monistic or dualistic. If it is monistic (all is one), it is open to the above criticisms of New Age. In addition, as Francis Schaeffer pointed out, these men have no satisfying explanation of how persons developed out of the impersonal.

> No one has presented an idea, let alone demonstrated it to be feasible, to explain how the impersonal beginning, plus time, plus chance, can give personality. We are distracted by a flourish of endless words, and lo, personality has appeared out of the hat! [23]

If 'the new story' is understood as dualistic (matter is ultimately unimportant; it is spirit that is important), there is the insurmountable problem that it is this dualistic thought that is largely responsible for man's misuse of nature in the first place.

As we approach the end of the second millennium, it is clear that many are disillusioned with a mechanistic, materialistic worldview and are struggling towards some kind of new, more spiritual philosophy. But neither New Age nor New Story provide the answers our personalness pleads for and our relation to nature demands. Is it not time we retraced our steps?

References

1. John Fowles, The Tree, quoted in *Trees for Life Calendar* 1991, The Trading Centre, Findhorn Foundation
2. *The Times*, 25 November 1989
3. Marilyn Ferguson, *The Aquarian Conspiracy*, (Paladin Grafton Books, 1988)
4. C. S. Lewis, *Miracles*, (Fontana, 1960), ps. 86,87
5. Shirley MacLaine, It's All in the Playing, quoted by James Sire in *The Universe Next Door*, (IVP, 1988), p. 170

6. Fritjof Capra, *The Turning Point: Science, Society and the Rising Culture*, (Fontana, 1982), p. 91

7. Shirley MacLaine, *Dancing in the Light*, (Bantam, 1986), p. 420

8. C. S. Lewis, *The Screwtape Letters*, (Collins, 1977), ps. 39,40

9. James Lovelock, quoted by Loren Wilkinson in 'New Age, New Consciousness and New Creation', *Tending the Garden*, ed. Wesley Granberg-Michaelson, (Eerdmans, 1987), p. 22

10. James Lovelock, *The Ages of Gaia*, (Oxford University Press, 1988), p. 19

11. *ibid.*, p. 212

12. Quoted by Loren Wilkinson in 'New Age, New Consciousness and New Creation', *Tending the Garden*, ed. Wesley Granberg-Michaelson, (Eerdmans, 1987), p. 23

13. Quoted by Jonathan Porritt in *The Coming of the Greens*, (Fontana, 1988), ps. 251,252

14. *ibid.* p. 246

15. *ibid.* p. 251

16. Paul Hawken, *The Magic of Findhorn*, (Fontana/Souvenir Press, 1988), p. 193

17. *ibid.* p. 127

18. Quoted by Tony Higton, The Environment as Religion' in *What is the New Age?*, (Hodder and Stoughton, 1990), p. 88

19. Sean McDonagh, *To Care For the Earth*, (Geoffrey Chapman, 1986), ps. 95,96

20. Santmire, *op. cit.*, p. 160

21. See Santmire, *op. cit.*, ps. 164-171

22. Humphrey Carpenter, *The Inklings*, (Unwin Paperbacks, 1981), p. 160

23. Francis Schaeffer, *The God Who Is There*, (Hodder and Stoughton, 1968), p. 88

CREATION IN CRISIS?

PART 3

LORD
OF
THE EARTH

CHAPTER FIVE

CREATED TO CARE

In turning to consider a Christian view of ecology, it is essential that we turn to authentic Christianity and not to what C. S. Lewis called "milk and water Christianity". One of the reasons why mainline Liberal Theology has been unable to respond adequately to the ecological crisis is because for over one hundred years it has been merely echoing non-Christian philosophy. If we want to find out what true Christianity is, we must turn to the Bible, the sourcebook recognised by all the major Christian traditions as the Word of God. So often the problem is not that men disagree as to what the Bible actually says, but that they disagree as to how what it says must be interpreted in light of their own particular philosophy or traditions.

It is my conviction that we will not find a real solution, not only to our ecological problems but to all our pressing problems, until we accept that the Creator who made the universe is speaking to us authoritatively and reliably in the Bible. That is the presupposition of the Bible itself. (A presupposition is an assumption which cannot be simply proved or disproved, but is essential to the establishing of any

argument or world-view.) Every world-view begins
with a presupposition or set of presuppositions.
Monism begins with the presupposition that 'All is
One'. Naturalism begins with the presupposition that
everything is explicable in terms of natural causes.
And Christianity begins with the presupposition that
the Creator is communicating truth to us in the Bible
- truth about himself, truth about the universe and
truth about us. Like all presuppositions this cannot
be simply proved or disproved, but I believe that when
we examine it and its implications we can discover
that it answers our questions, our problems and our
needs as nothing else does. Not least, it provides us
with a coherent, workable and beneficial view of
man's relationship to the rest of creation.

In the Beginning God

The Bible begins with the words, 'In the beginning
God created the heavens and the earth'.[1] From the
outset it is apparent that the Bible is theocentric -
God-centred. It does not begin with man. It begins
with God. The universe had a beginning, when God
created it. God had no beginning. He is 'from everlasting to everlasting'.[2] Throughout the Bible the
uniqueness of the being of God is stressed. He is the
only being who can say without qualification, 'I am
who I am'.[3] In contrast we must say with the Apostle
Paul that we are what we are only by the grace of God.[4]
God is the only self-existent being. He alone has life
in himself.[5] All other beings owe their existence to
him. Lynn White was totally wrong in saying that
Christianity is the most anthropocentric religion the

world has seen. That gives an absolutely false and misleading impression of what the Bible actually teaches. Men may have perverted Christianity into man-centred forms, but that is a completely different matter from what Christianity intrinsically is. That question is decided by what the Bible teaches.

Before the universe came into being, God was. Jesus refers to the complex life of the triune God as being there before the creation of the world:

> And now Father glorify me in your presence with the glory I had with you before the world began ... the glory you have given me because you loved me before the creation of the world.[6]

The Apostle John echoes the language of Genesis 1.1 in the opening words of his Gospel:

> In the beginning was the Word and the Word was with God and the Word was God. He was with God in the beginning. Through him all things were made; without him nothing was made that has been made.[7]

Now all this tells us things fundamental to a proper understanding of God's relation to the universe. God is not part of the universe. He is not merely the force or power or energy of the universe. He is not the soul of the universe. He is *sui generis* - one of a kind. He is distinct from the universe for he created it and he existed before it and independently of it. But equally what God tells us about himself and his creation of the world stresses that the universe is not part of God, it is not an extension of God, not a dream of God. He made it, he created it, he brought it into existence. It has a real distinct existence of its own. Therefore any kind of pantheism, any confusing of the Creator with the creation, is ruled out.

Order out of Chaos

However, although God is independent of the creation, the creation is not independent of God. The Bible reveals theism not deism.

According to the deistic view, God wound up the universe like a clock and set it going to work according to its own immutable laws, or in more modern terms, he caused the big bang and everything has evolved from there according to an internal dynamic.

But the Bible makes it clear that when God created the universe, whether by the big bang or some other event or series of events, he continued to maintain an intimate connection with the universe. Indeed we can say that if he did not sustain the universe continuously, it would either descend into chaos or cease to exist altogether: 'The Son is the radiance of God's glory and the exact representation of his being, sustaining all things by his powerful word' - 'He is before all things and in him all things hold together'. [8]

God's sustaining power extends from the stars in the heavens to the sparrows on the earth:

Lift up your eyes and look to the heavens: Who created all these? He who brings out the starry

host one by one, and calls them each by name.
Because of his great power and mighty strength,
not one of them is missing. [9]

Are not two sparrows sold for a penny? Yet
not one of them will fall to the ground apart
from the will of your Father. [10]

The method by which God sustains all things is
ultimately mysterious to us, but it may be that modern
mathematics and physics are now coming near to
recognising that mysterious process. In both the
concept of chaos in mathematics and in quantum
physics there is a growing openness to the possibility
of God being at work at a level incomprehensible to
us. Research mathematician, Ian Stewart, takes the
title of his book *Does God Play Dice?* from the famous
words of Albert Einstein to Max Born, 'You believe
in the God who plays dice, and I in complete law and
order'. After showing that we cannot accurately
predict the outcome of many processes, ranging from
the weather to population changes in ecology, he
concludes:

Either God is playing dice, or He's playing a
deeper game that we have yet to fathom. I
agree with Einstein. I like the second idea - the
deeper game which we don't understand yet - a
lot more. Now . . . we've finally realised that
deterministic chaos is responsible for a great
deal of the observed randomness in classical
mechanics. Might quantum chaos be responsible for observed randomness in quantum me-

chanics? Can we now fathom out God's deeper
game? Not at the moment. If there is a deeper
game, it's still too deep for us teachable apes.
We're in desperate need of a True Man to put
us on the right lines ...

Quantum uncertainty may be like this. An
infinitely intelligent being with perfect senses -
God, Vast Intellect, or Deep Thought - might
actually be able to predict exactly when a given
atom of radium will decay, a given electron shift
in its orbit. But with our limited intellects and
imperfect senses, we may never be able to find
the trick. [11]

Whether these new developments in mathematics
and science turn out to be saying what they seem to be
saying about the finiteness of man and the possibility
of a sustaining work of the Creator remains to be
seen. What is certain is that the Bible stresses the
reality of this sustaining power of God. Although the
creation is, of necessity, distinct from the Creator, it
depends upon him, not only for its existence through
his act of creation, but also for his continuous involvement in sustaining his creatures. This involvement
takes place not only at the imperceptible-to-us level
of God's holding the particles of the physical universe
together, but also at the level of God's providence for
his creatures. The Bible is full of references to God's
caring for the creation. Psalm 104 is one of the most
celebrated examples:

He waters the mountains from his upper chambers;
　　the earth is satisfied by the fruit of his work.
He makes grass grow for the cattle,
　　and plants for man to cultivate -
　　bringing forth food from the earth:
wine that gladdens the heart of man,
　　oil to make his face shine,
　　and bread that sustains his heart.
The trees of the Lord are well watered,
　　the cedars of Lebanon that he planted.
There the birds make their nests;
　　the stork has its home in the pine trees.
The high mountains belong to the wild goats;
　　the crags are a refuge for the conies.

The moon marks off the seasons,
　　and the sun knows when to go down.
You bring darkness, it becomes night,
　　and all the beasts of the forests prowl.
The lions roar for their prey
　　and seek their food from God.
The sun rises and they steal away;
　　they return and lie down in their dens.
Then man goes out to his work,
　　to his labour until the evening.

How many are your works, O Lord!
　　In wisdom you made them all;
　　the earth is full of your creatures.
There is the sea, vast and spacious,
　　teeming with creatures beyond number -
　　living things both large and small.

There the ships go to and fro,
     and the leviathan which you formed to frolic there.
These all look to you
     to give them their food at the proper time. [12]

Delight in Nature

Here we see not only the bare doctrine of God's
providence for his creatures, important though that is
in itself. We see a delight in the creatures in themselves and in their relationship to God. Nor is it only
creatures which may be deemed useful to man that
are considered. Storks, wild goats, conies, lions and
whales all give cause for wonder and delight. As C. S.
Lewis pointed out, this nature poetry of Israel was
something almost unique in the ancient world. It was
all the more remarkable, he held, for being created by
people who were not cushioned, as many of us are,
from the real natural world:

Of course this appreciation of, almost this sym-
pathy with, creatures useless or hurtful or wholly
irrelevant to man, is not our modern "kindness
to animals". That is a virtue most easily practised
by those who have never, tired and hungry, had
to work with animals for a bare living, and who
inhabit a country where all dangerous wild beasts
have been exterminated.... When a hard-worked
shepherd or carter remains kind to animals his
back may well be patted; not ours. [13]

But the main point is that the Bible teaches that
knowing God as creator and sustainer of nature, does

not empty nature of significance, as New Agers and other pantheists would have us believe; rather the reverse. C. S. Lewis comments,

> By emptying Nature of divinity - or, let us say, of divinities - you may fill her with Deity, for she is now the bearer of messages. There is a sense in which Nature-worship silences her - as if a child or a savage were so impressed with the postman's uniform that he omitted to take in the letters. [14]

For the Christian, 'The world is charged with the grandeur of God', as poet Gerard Manley Hopkins put it. The universe is not less mysterious, majestic and marvellous when you believe God created it and is sustaining it, it is more so. It was no accident that it was the Dutch artists in Reformation Holland who really started painting nature in a realistic way. The rediscovered Bible taught them that nature was important in itself because God had made it and was sustaining it. So we see that there is no basis for a disdain or disregard of nature in the Bible. Here again we see that Lynn White, and those who have followed him, have a total misconception of what biblical Christianity actually says about nature. White stated:

> To a Christian a tree can be no more than a physical fact. The whole concept of the sacred grove is alien to Christianity and to the ethos of the West. For nearly two millenia Christian missionaries have been chopping down sacred

groves, which are idolatrous because they assume spirit in nature. [15]

Certainly sacred groves were cut down, and there is good biblical warrant for so doing. God commanded Gideon to cut down the Asherah pole which formed part of the false fertility worship of the goddess Asherah. [16] But the very fact that he was then commanded to utilise the wood of the Asherah pole in the worship of the true God demonstrates that there is nothing evil in the natural wood itself. The evil lay in the wrong use to which men put it. The groves were cut down, not because of a hatred of nature, but because of a love of nature as God created it and a love of the God who created it. It is the pagan worship of nature that is a perversion, not the Christian delight in nature.

Do we really want to go back to the pagan nature worship of Canaan and all that was involved in it, including human sacrifice? The tragedy is that we have already set out on the return journey. It is no coincidence that many involved in the Green movement have a very low view of the value of human life. While ostensibly placing a high value on life in general, they see little wrong with the killing of unborn children in abortion. Indeed some of them see this as a necessary sacrifice on the part of the human race to reduce the human population and its destructive impact on the environment.

Mother Goddess?
In addition, must not the emphasis in liberal theology,

feminism and deep ecology on the need to see God as feminine be seen against this biblical background of implacable opposition to the worship of nature fertility goddesses? This emphasis is yet another example of the bankruptcy of liberal theology in its slavish echoing of the views of the world. The church is called to faithfully deliver the Word of God irrespective of how unpopular it may be deemed to be.

What we do find in the Bible is that feminine analogies as well as masculine ones are used of God. The Spirit of God hovered or brooded over the waters in creation (Genesis 1:2), God loves his people more than even a mother loves the baby at her breast (Isaiah 49:15), and Jesus longed to gather the children of Jerusalem together as a hen gathers her chicks under her wings (Luke 13:34). The point of these analogies is not that we are to conceive of God as goddess, any more than we are to conceive of him as a woman or a man or a hen! The point of the feminine analogies is that God's love is reflected in maternal feminine love as well as in the masculine love of father and husband. God's love is greater by far than any human or animal love, so these are all pale, though true, reflections of his great love, and can all serve as analogies, each adding a dimension to our understanding of God which otherwise would be missing.

Nevertheless, the fact remains that Jesus commands us to address God as Father, not Mother (Matthew 6.9), throughout the Bible God describes himself by the use of masculine not feminine pronouns, Jesus is the Son not daughter of God and he was incarnate as a man not a woman. God obviously considered it important to reveal himself in masculine terms rather than feminine and for us to worship him in those terms. Although the reasons for this may not be wholly apparent to us, yet the history of attempts to introduce the Goddess concept shows that the effect has always been to corrupt the truth.

It happened in ancient Israel, it has happened with the virtual deification of Mary in popular Roman Catholicism and it has clearly happened in liberal theology. Theologian Sallie McFague argues that in an ecological and nuclear age we must abandon the biblical teaching about the relationship of God to the world, which she calls the monarchical concept, in favour of the concept of the world as God's body and God as Mother, Lover and Friend. Apart from the fact that the concept of the world as God's body is pantheistic and unbiblical, the whole tendency of her theology is to eviscerate the gospel. In discussing 'God as Mother' and 'God as Lover', she says:

> Discussions of agape as definitive of divine love have, unfortunately, usually focussed on redemption, not creation, and as a result have stressed the disinterested character of God's love, which can overlook the sin in the sinners and love them anyway. In other words, even although we are worthless, we are loved - but disinterestedly. Needless to say, this is a sterile and unattractive view of divine love and a view that most of us would not settle for even as a description of human love . . .

Do we want to be loved in spite of who we are or because of who we are? That is, if we are talking about the greatest love there is - God's love - is it not far greater to be loved as God's beloved than as a rebellious sinner? [17]

This may be what we want. However, the question is not what we want, but what we need and what God has provided. The message of the Gospel is indubitably that God loves us although we do not deserve to be loved:

But God demonstrates his own love for us in this: While we were still sinners, Christ died for us.

This is love: not that we loved God, but that he loved us and sent his Son as an atoning sacrifice for our sins.

It is not the healthy who need a doctor, but the sick. I have not come to call the righteous, but sinners to repentance. [18]

But what is so amazing about God's love is that he loves the undeserving as if they did deserve his love. He loves the church as his children and as his bride: 'As a father has compassion on his children, so the Lord has compassion on those who fear him' (Psalm 103.13). 'Husbands, love your wives, just as Christ loved the church and gave himself up for her' (Ephesians 5.25).

It is clear that the attempt by McFague and others

to create new models of God in terms of a Mother has more in common with New Age than the New Testament. It lays the emphasis on self-centred human desires, not God's revelation and redemption in Christ; and on a pantheistic concept of God's relation to the world as his body, not the biblical concept of the world being distinct from but dependent on God. Whatever such a theology is, it is not Christianity.

Creature-Kings

A right understanding of the Bible's teaching about God's relation to the universe in creating, sustaining and providing is essential to building up a full view of the ecological implications of Christianity. However, there is an even more controversial area, and that is the question of man's relationship to nature. As we saw earlier (in Chapter 3), if there is one thing many in the Green Movement know about Christianity it is that the Bible teaches that God gave man dominion over the rest of creation. This is construed in a wholly negative and destructive way.

What exactly is the biblical teaching on the relation of man to nature? The first thing we must face is that this is not merely a two-way relationship - man and nature. It is a three-way relationship - God, man and nature.

From all that we have already discovered about God's sovereignty, it is clear that there can be no such thing as a relationship between any of his creatures that does not involve him. This is where it becomes obvious that the idea of man's dominion over nature giving him an autonomous power is a deistic or humanist idea, not a Christian one. Whatever this dominion is, it is defined and regulated by God, not by man. Man's dominion must be seen in the context of all that the Bible has to say concerning this three-way relationship.

There is the fact that man is both the fellow-creature of other creatures and their ruler. Francis Schaeffer expressed this memorably with reference to God as 'the infinite, personal God'. The God who reveals himself in the Bible is unique in that he is infinite-personal. By contrast, the pagan gods are personal, but limited; and the god of pantheism is unlimited, but impersonal. The Christian concept of God, which we have learned from the Bible, is absolutely unique. He is both infinite and personal. This has important implications for our understanding of man's relationship to nature. This is how Schaeffer expressed it:

On the side of His infinity there is the great chasm. He creates all things and He alone is Creator. Everything else is created. Only He is Infinite and only He is the Creator; everything else is the creature and finite. Only He is independent; everything else is dependent. So man, the animal, the flower and the machine, in the biblical viewpoint, are equally separated from God, in that He created them all. On the side of infinity man is as separated from God as is the machine.

. . . But there is another side - the Personal. Here the animal, the flower and the machine are below the chasm. On the side of God's Infinity everything else is finite and equally separated from God; but on the side of his Personality God has created man in His own image. [19]

This is the biblical balance which we must constantly bear in mind as we consider a Christian view of ecology. On the one hand humans share creaturehood and limitedness with all other creatures, but on the other hand, humans are unique - God created us in his own image.

The emphasis that we share creaturehood and limitedness with all other creatures is a necessary corrective to man's pride - the tendency to man-centredness. We cannot have a man-centred view if we have a biblical view. God has created us, yes, but he is also the Creator and Sustainer of every other creature. He has purposes and plans for all his creatures, some of which may be revealed to us and which may involve us, but some of which may not. After he had created the whole universe, but before he created man, 'God saw that it was good'. The Hebrew word translated 'good' means both good and beautiful. Nature is good and beautiful in the eyes of God quite apart from man. So we must treat all creatures with respect for they are ultimately God's, not ours. 'The earth is the LORD's and everything in it' (Psalm 24.1). 'The glory of the LORD fills the whole earth' (Numbers 14.21). God owns the earth, and the earth is full of his glory. Therefore we must treat all of his creatures with care. We must seek to ensure that we treat them according to his directions not according to our own whims.

Although it is thus clear that human beings share creaturehood and limitedness with all other creatures, the Bible also teaches that our primary relationship is not with other creatures but with God. We are uniquely created in the image of God. Humans alone are created as personal beings with the God-like abilities of speech, moral judgement and creativity. Of particular note in the present context is the fact that our being in God's image is linked closely with our dominion over creation.

> Then God said, "Let us make man in our image, in our likeness, and let them rule over the fish of the sea and the birds of the air, over the livestock, over all the earth and over all the creatures that move along the ground." So God created man in his own image, in the image of God he created him; male and female he created them. God blessed them and said to them, "Be fruitful and increase in number; fill the earth and subdue it."[20]

Because we are made in God's image, we have been given authority over the other creatures. We are kings of creation. But nowhere is there any indication that man has a 'licence to conduct himself as the earth's worst pest'. Rather the reverse. God placed clear limitations on man's rule. For instance, man was not allowed to eat anything he liked. His diet was to be limited to plants and fruit. It is true that this limitation was later lifted after the Flood, but the point is that it was God's decision to limit or not to limit, not man's. Similarly God placed Adam in the Garden of Eden not to do as he pleased, but 'to work it and take care of it' (Genesis 2.15) and even in it there was one tree, the fruit of which he was not allowed to eat.

The point is that although God has given the earth to man (Psalm 115.16), it is not an absolute and unconditional gift. The earth still remains the LORD's. One is reminded of the words of Samuel Rutherford in *Lex Rex:* 'Power is a birthright of the people, borrowed from them: they may let it out for their good and may resume it when a man is drunk with it.' He was speaking of the political power of the Stewart kings, but the same principle applies to the power of man over nature. God has given him that power and He may recall it or modify it as He will. The environment in which man moves in the Bible constantly implies that man is answerable to God. Man is God's gardener, shepherd and steward. One day we will have to give an account of how we have discharged our stewardship.

The fact remains that man's authority over nature, though a delegated authority, is an authority nonetheless. The Christian should not be embarrassed or defensive about that. After all, everyone concerned for the well-being of the earth recognises the crucial role that the human race must play. Every Green pressure group exhorts us to change our personal, social, agricultural and industrial practices for the good of the whole planet. They present programmes, strategies and policies towards that end. They take for granted man's right to do these things, to take this lead.

The vital question is: What gives us this right? If we are merely one species among many, why should we arrogate to ourselves the role of being the earth's policeman? If, as some believe, dolphins and whales are better than us, should we not wait for them to do something about the ecological crisis, and meanwhile carry on doing what comes naturally to us? Or if Gaia is in ultimate control, maybe we should leave it up to her and not interfere. Of course, no rational person suggests any such thing. It is obvious that man exercises dominion over the earth. The Bible alone gives the explanation for that: man is created in the image of God. God has given him this right. The only question is: How are we exercising that right - for good or evil?

References

1. Genesis 1.1
2. Psalm 90.2
3. Exodus 3.14
4. 1 Corinthians 15.10
5. John 5.26
6. John 17.5,24
7. John 1.1-3
8. Hebrews 1.3, Colossians 1.17
9. Isaiah 40.25
10. Matthew 10.29
11. Ian Stewart, *Does God Play Dice?*, (Penguin, 1990), ps. 293,300
12. Psalm 104.13-27

13. C. S. Lewis, *Reflections on the Psalms*, (Fontana, 1961), p. 72

14. ibid. p.71

15. Lynn White, *op. cit.*, p.82

16. Judges 6.25,26

17. Sallie McFague, *Models of God*, (SCM Press, 1987), ps. 102,133

18. Romans 5.8, 1 John 4.10, Luke 5.31,32

19. Francis Schaeffer, *Pollution and the Death of Man*, ps. 35,36

20. Genesis 1.26-28

CHAPTER SIX

THE GATES OF EDEN

One of the major problems that confronts us in Green issues is this: Is the world in its present condition normal or abnormal? I do not just mean whether present phenomena like deserts or peat bogs are as they have always been, but whether global conditions, including human attitudes and action particularly, are normal or not. It seems to me to be an assumption of the Greens that the world is not normal. There exists somewhere a specification of a perfect world and their aim is to match the present imperfect world to that perfect specification.

The problem is whether such a position is consistent with the prevailing New-Age-type world-view among many Greens. It is the problem confronting all pantheistic monism. If all is one and all is God, how can anything be abnormal? The world is as it was in the beginning and evermore shall be. Man is as he was in the beginning and evermore shall be. As in Hindu India there is no impetus to change the world for the better. Pantheism has never been able to find an answer to the question of mass-murderer Charles Manson: If all is one and God is one, what is evil?

Oxford scholar R. C. Zaehner, an expert in Eastern religion, commented:

> Charles Manson was absolutely sane: he had been there, where there is neither good nor evil ... If the ultimate truth ... is that "All is One" and "One is All" ... then have we any right to blame Charles Manson? For seen from the point of view of the eternal Now, he did nothing at all. [1]

This is because the pantheist refuses to accept the concept of the Fall: that man is not now as he was originally created; the world is not now as it was originally created. It is this Christian concept of the Fall which we find in the Bible that provides the only solid basis on which to say the world is abnormal and man is abnormal. Taken together with what the Bible teaches about God's grace and man's responsibility, this gives us the only consistent foundation from which to work to change the world for the better.

Distorted Image

The Bible clearly teaches that man is not now as he was originally created. But that statement needs clarification. This does not mean that man's constitution as made in the image of God has totally changed. After the Fall man is still described as being in the image of God.[2] He is still a personal being distinguished from the animals by a God-likeness that is expressed in all the abilities that equip him to rule over the other creatures. Jesus said that a man is more valuable than a sheep and that his disciples are worth more than many sparrows. [3] However, what did change in the Fall was man's spiritual and moral nature in its totality. Whereas God declared the original creation, including man, to be very good, with the Fall man became corrupt in all his faculties - mind, will and emotions - and in all his communication and action. [4]

It is sometimes thought difficult to reconcile these two biblical emphases - that humans are both made in the image of God and yet now totally corrupt. But let us imagine a father and son. The father is a great artist and his son inherits his artistic abilities. However, whereas the father produced works of great beauty, depth and power, the son uses all his abilities to produce works of shallow and hideous pornography. We can say that the son is the image of his father. The ability is there, but it is now totally perverted. That is an analogy of man being now the corrupted image of God. This corruption of man is called 'total depravity'. That is a term that is usually misunderstood. It does not mean that everyone is as bad as he might possibly be. It means quite simply that there is no aspect of our humanity that escapes the pollution of sin. Our relationship with God, our relationship with other human beings, our relationship with ourselves and our relationship with nature are all corrupted.

Before the Fall all these relationships are portrayed in Genesis 2 as in perfect harmony. In the Fall all these relationships are disrupted. Of particular relevance for our present purpose is the fact that the Fall involved not only the spiritual, the social and the psychological, but also the ecological. Indeed the very test that God devised to test human obedience involved man's relationship with nature. In fact it was a test to see if man would accept that his dominion over nature was a delegated and a limited dominion. God said, 'You are free to eat from any tree in the garden; but you must not eat from the tree of the knowledge of good and evil, for when you eat of it you will surely die.'[5] This again underlines the uniqueness of man, for to no other creature did God give such a test of obedience. Man is a moral being who can know good and evil from the side of good, if he chooses to obey God, or from the side of evil, if he chooses to disobey. However, the main point is whether man would recognise God as God, or seek a dominion greater than that given to him.

We all know what happened. Man disobeyed and has been in a state of rebellion ever since. But the manner in which he fell is crucially important for the present debate. He fell because he yielded to temptation and the temptation came in the arena not only of man's relationship with God but of man's relationship with nature. God chose a tree as the test. There is no indication that there was anything out of the ordinary about the tree in itself. We are simply told its distinct position - it was in the middle of the Garden of Eden - and we are told that God designated it by a particular name - it was the tree of the knowledge of good and evil. The question was whether man would treat this particular part of creation as God had commanded him to treat it.

The creation was also involved in that the temptation was mediated through a snake. No one can deny that there is mystery here. But the indications are that apart from one major distinctive, this was an ordinary snake. The major distinctive was that this snake spoke! When we piece together the information given us in the rest of the Bible, it becomes clear that this particular snake was grotesquely and perversely possessed by Satan in order to tempt Adam and Eve. So again we see that nature was involved. It was abused by Satan to mislead man. It must be said at this point that in Christian thought Satan is not an equal and opposite power to God. The indications in the Bible are that he was created perfect by God as an angel or archangel, yet in pride he rebelled. [6] There was a Fall in the angelic world before there was a Fall in the human world.

New Age Temptation

However, it is the terms of Satan's temptation that are of particular interest here (see Genesis 3). It is fascinating that the thinking expressed is reflected in some aspects of New Age thought. His first stratagem was to cast doubt on God's Word: "Did God really say, 'You must not eat from any tree in the garden'?" (v.1) Specifically he cast doubt on God's giving any absolute moral command to man. This is one of the characteristics that New Age has inherited from Eastern thought and is widely accepted now in the West. There is no such thing as absolute truth. Everybody has their own view of reality. This is how American scientist and author John Lilly sees it:

> In the province of the mind, what is believed to
> be true is or becomes true, within limits to be
> found experientially and experimentally. These
> limits are further limits to be transcended. In
> the province of the mind there are no limits. [7]

Not only does this relativism destroy the possibility
of real communication between persons. It destroys
the possibility of knowing the truth concerning the
universe and our obligations concerning it. By contrast, the fact that God speaks to us and that he speaks
to us truly is the basis of all knowledge, all morality
and all right treatment of the creation.

Satan's second stratagem was to deny death: 'You
will not surely die' (v.4). The full implications of death
in Biblical thought are not only physical but spiritual.
Death is ultimately separation from God, and God
promised death as the penalty for disobedience. But
Satan denied the consequences of sin and the reality
of death, physical, spiritual and eternal. Similarly,
New Agers deny the reality of death. There is no
possibility of anyone being ultimately separated from
God. They hold that we will all be absorbed back into
God (or the One). They also remove the uniqueness
of physical death and therefore the uniqueness of life
through their belief in reincarnation. The implication of such thinking is that it does not really matter
how you live now. No irrevocable consequences will
follow upon your disobedience of God's commands,
even if these concern nature. In total contra-distinc-
tion to this is the Christian view of life which holds
that our actions are incredibly significant. Disobedi-

ence of God's law leads to death: 'Man is destined to die once, and after that to face judgement' (Hebrews 9.27). We are answerable to God for all our sins, including our sins against the rest of creation.

Satan's third and final stratagem was that they should deify themselves: 'your eyes will be opened, and you will be like God, knowing good and evil' (v.5). He promised that disobeying God's command, far from leading to death, would lead to the enlightenment of divinity. This is precisely what New Age thinking promises today. This is largely why it is so appealing to self-centred man. But this is also exactly why it is totally useless as a world-view to solve our ecological crisis. Contra Lynn White, it is not Christianity but New Age thought that is the most anthropocentric worldview the world has ever seen. What could be more anthropocentric than proclaiming man's deity? It was in this very act of placing self at the centre instead of God that the human race fell.

Fallen World

The Fall had certain immediate consequences. All man's relationships were disrupted, including his relationship with nature. The perfect harmony and balance of God's original creation is destroyed:

Cursed is the ground because of you; through painful toil you will eat of it all the days of your life. It will produce thorns and thistles for you, and you will eat the plants of the field. By the sweat of your brow you will eat your food until you return to the ground, since from it you were

106

taken; for dust you are and to dust you will return. [8]

There are two things we must notice here. The earth is cursed because of man's sin. It is man's sinful, self-centred, disobedient attitude that has disrupted the perfect harmony. But also we must not ignore the fact that it is God who pronounced this curse upon the earth. It is part of the justly imposed penalty for sin. God does not allow man to sin with impunity. This has continued to be the state of affairs in the world ever since. To answer our question at the beginning of this chapter, the world is not now in its normal condition, nor is man. Neither are as they were created. In the area of ecology we are constantly struggling against the ravages of man's sin in the world. And man in his sinful state cannot properly deal with the situation. All his attempts are vitiated by pride, lust and greed. Man's dominion over the earth has been corrupted.

The early chapters of Genesis make this abundantly clear. The Cainite line of the human race forged ahead with the subduing of the earth in city-building, livestock-rearing and metalwork. But theirs was a dominion that was vitiated by pride and violence from the beginning, which eventually corrupted the whole human race bar one family. God brought the Flood to destroy the whole earth because of its almost total moral and spiritual pollution. 'Now the earth was corrupt in God's sight and was full of violence. God saw how corrupt the earth had become, for all the people on earth had corrupted their ways' (Genesis 6.11,12).

This pattern of human sin leading to destruction of nature and the judgement of God is repeated many times throughout the Bible. A few examples will suffice. The sins for which God exiled Israel from the land include not only the worship of the false nature gods and goddesses of Canaan, but also their refusal to treat the land as God had commanded.

> The land enjoyed its Sabbath rests; all the time of its desolation it rested, until the seventy years were completed in fulfilment of the word of the LORD spoken by Jeremiah (2 Chronicles 36.21).

Part of God's law had included a command to let the land lie fallow every seventh year. In Judah's pride and greed and their embracing of the fertility deities of Canaan they had neglected this care for the land. This led to the inevitable consequence of God's judgement.

In a passage speaking of the judgement and downfall of the King of Babylon (the very Babylon which God had used to punish Judah) he is described as 'the man who made the world a desert' (Isaiah 14.17). Similarly, in the Book of Daniel the Roman empire is spoken of as a fourth kingdom (after the Babylonian, Persian and Greek empires): 'It will be different from all the other kingdoms and will devour the whole earth, trampling it down and crushing it' (Daniel 7.23). It is interesting to note in passing that in terms of biblical prophecy this fourth kingdom will continue in some form to the end of the world, but will be destroyed by Christ. In a passage describing God's final judgement of the world in the Book of Revelation it is said that, 'The time has come for judging the dead ... and for destroying those who destroy the earth' (Revelation 11:18). It is thus clear that the Biblical view is that human sin is responsible for the destruction of the earth and God is judging and will judge us for it.

Therefore, in Christian terms the ecological crisis is a moral problem not a metaphysical or an epistemological problem. It is to do with what man does (sin) not with who he is (image of God) or how he gains knowledge (revelation, reason and faith). The error of New Age thinking and much Green thinking is the belief that the answer lies in the abandoning of Christian metaphysics and epistemology. They refuse to consider the radical nature of man's own inner pollution and instead try to find the solution in pantheistic monism and intuitive or occult thinking, in spite of the fact that societies where these have been the norm have been socially oppressive and ecologically destructive. Lecturer in religious studies, John Drane, comments:

> For this is the outlook that has consistently produced some of the most oppressive forms of social organisation that the world has ever seen. Societies in which women have been regularly abused, children on occasion have been sacrificed, and a small number of people claiming superior spiritual knowledge have terrified everybody else ...

Thailand's tropical rain forests were being

systematically destroyed at an alarming rate for almost half a century before anything at all started happening in Brazil - again by the devotees of a so called 'holistic' religion. Japan - with a very similar traditional worldview - is the one country in the world that allows the routine slaughter of whales and dolphins. [9]

However, the Bible not only shows that it is human disobedience to God's law that has caused the problem. It also reveals that God has acted to deal decisively with human disobedience and to provide salvation. We must now look at that salvation and, while we must look at it in its specific application to human beings, we will also see that it has decided implications for the rest of creation.

Seed and Sacrifice

When the creation started to go wrong in the Fall, God did not unmake the world. The challenge to his moral government of the universe had to be met. The breaking of the law required justice. The truly staggering thing, however, is that God did not immediately and fully implement the threatened punishment, 'You will surely die'. He did not immediately sentence Adam and Eve to hell. The reason was not that he was being unjust and untrue to his word, but that he was staying his hand in mercy. The great puzzle of the Old Testament is: How can God be both just and merciful? That question reverberates down the centuries, and although it was not fully answered until the New Testament, there were clear indications in the Old Testament of the solution.

We read that right after the Fall God did two things which are pointers to his plan of mercy. He promised that an offspring (or seed) of Eve's would destroy Satan's power (Genesis 3:15) and he clothed Adam and Eve with skins (v.21). These two strands of seed and sacrifice run right through the Old Testament until they are twined together in Jesus Christ. We must look at each of these in turn. In the first place, there is the emphasis that the hope of the world is focussed on a man, a particular man, the emphasis that later came to be known as the Messianic hope. There would be an offspring, a seed, a descendant. At first it was the seed of the woman who would crush the head of Satan. Then it was the seed of Abraham through whom all nations on earth would be blessed (Genesis 22:18). Latterly it was the seed of David who would have an everlasting kingdom (2 Samuel 7:12ff).

This emphasis on the seed is bound up with another central Biblical emphasis - the emphasis on covenant. Indeed the whole of the Bible can be seen as covenant. That is why the two parts of the Bible are known as Old and New Testaments (or Covenants). Covenant is fundamentally a promise. God promises that he will be our God, that he will save us and give us an inheritance. That is why the promise of a descendant is bound up with covenant. However, although covenant is sovereignly initiated by God, a human response is also involved. These aspects are seen most clearly in the foundational Old Testament administration of the covenant - the covenant made with Abraham. God promised to be his God and the God of his descendants, he promised the inheritance of the land of Canaan, he promised a descendant through whom all nations on earth would be blessed, and Abraham responded in faith and obedience. [10]

Promised Land

One aspect of the covenant has particular relevance for any attempt to work out a Christian ecology. I refer to God's promising the land of Canaan to his people. In course of time this promise was fulfilled. But when the land was given to Israel it was not an absolute gift or a transfer of property from God to man.

As Meredith Kline and others have shown, the form of God's covenant with man, particularly the covenant with Israel, is in the form of a vassal treaty. [11] In contemporary history a great king would make a treaty (literally 'cut a covenant') with a vassal king, imposing certain obligations on him and his people. This is clearly the kind of covenant that God made with Israel. God specifically says, 'the land is mine and you are but aliens and my tenants' (Leviticus 25:23). Thus we see again that just as the original dominion of man was not an absolute dominion but was subject to God's commands, so the gift of the land to a redeemed people did not involve a transfer of sovereign right, but was subject to God's law. Biblical scholar Christopher Wright comments:

It is the belief that God owns the land and demands accountability in the use of it from his 'tenants' that generates the literal 'earthiness' of Old Testament ethics. Nothing you can do in, on or with the land is outside the sphere of God's moral inspection. From major issues of the defence of the national territory down to how you prune your fruit trees, every area of life is included. [12]

There were laws that established social justice, by placing a limit on a 'free market economy' with regard to the tenancy of the land. No one would be allowed to buy up land and keep it in perpetuity, thus dominating land use, because every fifty years land returned to the original family at the Year of Jubilee. There were laws that forbade a rapacious exploitation of the land. The land was to be left fallow every seventh year to provide for the poor and for wildlife. Fruit trees were not to be cut down for seigeworks in war-time. The reason given for the latter command has a strangely modern ring to it - 'the tree of the field is man's life'. We are discovering afresh that we despoil God's creation at our peril.

There were also laws that protected wildlife. If eggs were taken from a nest, it was forbidden to take the mother bird as well. She had to be allowed to go free (the implication being that she would be able to raise another brood). There were laws concerning the integrity of God's creation. It was forbidden to mate different kinds of animals (this has relevance to areas of genetic engineering today). There were laws concerning the welfare of farm animals. The ox and the donkey were entitled to a day of rest as well as people, and lost and fallen animals were to be helped. This is why it is said in the Book of Proverbs, 'A righteous man cares for the needs of his animal'. [13]

The Lamb of God

We must now return and consider the other strand of Old Testament teaching in which the redemptive love of God is seen - sacrifice. The first animal that was killed for man's sake was not to feed him but to cover him. Before the Fall there was no shame in nakedness, but as soon as Adam and Eve disobeyed God they knew shame for the first time and they tried to cover themselves with leaves. God showed that this self-covering was totally inadequate. To deal with sin and its consequences was a far more costly affair. They had to be clothed with skin. An animal's life had to be sacrificed. This was developed later through the simple sacrifices of Abel, Noah and Abraham into the complex sacrificial system instituted at Sinai.

In that system it is made clear that one of the main purposes of sacrifice was to atone for (literally to cover) sin. Only by an animal taking the place of the guilty sinner and dying in his place could sin be covered and the sinner accepted by God. In this way the sacrificial animal typified Christ who is 'the Lamb of God who takes away the sin of the world' (John 1:29). It is Christ who is the real sacrifice for sin, the one who gives his life as a ransom for many (Mark 10:45).

The existence of animal sacrifice in the Bible has often been adduced as evidence that Christianity has a low view of animal life. In fact the opposite is true.

It is because the animal is considered so near to man that it can serve as a substitute. Although it is not made in the image of God, yet it has blood and the breath of life in it. The same words that are used of man's life, 'soul' and 'spirit', are used of animal life. Similarly, the fact that the animal typifies Christ gives it the highest value that can be given. When you come to believe that Christ is the Lamb of God who died for you, your view of the ordinary lamb is higher, not lower. In addition, the fact that animals were used in sacrifice had a profound impact upon the use of animal meat for food. From creation and even after the Fall man was not permitted to eat meat. Indeed it may be legitimately questioned whether any animal was carnivorous before the Fall. God gave only plants and fruit to both men and animals for food (Genesis 1:29,30, 3:17,18).

Be that as it may, from the time of the Flood, God permitted man to eat meat. However, there was a significant condition - 'But you must not eat meat that has its lifeblood still in it' (Genesis 9:4). Whatever else was involved, this meant that man was not permitted to hack meat from a living animal. The animal had to be properly slaughtered by draining its blood. Later, in the covenant at Sinai, the connection with sacrifice is made clear. The Israelites were forbidden to eat blood, because God had given them the blood of the animal for atonement on the altar (Leviticus 17:10-12). This had an implication for the slaughtering of any animal, even if hunted for food. The life of every animal had to be treated with respect. There was something awesome about the killing of an animal.

This is something that most of us are sheltered from in this age of industrialised farming and slaughterhouse technology. You have a different perspective when you have to kill an animal with a knife. Every year on the hill sheep farm where my father was a shepherd, all the shepherds of the neighbouring farms would gather for 'the clipping', the sheepshearing, when thousands of sheep would be sheared. Preparation for the big day involved the slaughter of a sheep to feed the workers. When I was older I helped my father to do it. It was not an easy thing to do. All the instincts of the shepherd are to preserve the life of his flock. There was very much the feeling that something valuable was being sacrificed for our sake. It is only permissible to use the Bible's teaching to justify man's use of animals for meat or for medical research, if we also take the biblical view that we are sacrificing something precious in the sight of God and that we are answerable for any misuse to God who will one day judge us.

Redeemed Creation

So far we have considered mainly Old Testament themes connected with God's mercy to the world. However, it is in the New Testament that not only do these themes reach their fulfilment in Christ, but staggering new insights are given to themes only hinted at in the Old Testament. Here it becomes clear that the promised descendant of the woman, of Abraham and of David, although true man, is also the eternal Son of God. He is the very One who created the universe and sustains it by his power:

He is the image of the invisible God, the firstborn
over all creation. For by him all things were
created: things in heaven and on earth, visible
and invisible, whether thrones or powers or
rulers or authorities; all things were created by
him and for him. He is before all things and in
him all things hold together. And he is the head
of the body, the church; he is the beginning and
the firstborn from among the dead, so that in
everything he might have the supremacy. For
God was pleased to have all his fulness dwell in
him, and through him to reconcile to himself all
things, whether things on earth or things in
heaven, by making peace through his blood
shed on the cross. [14]

In addition, we here see that he is the One who by
his death not only saves individual sinners, but recon-
ciles the whole universe to God. This is not to say that
every individual human being will be saved. The Bible
clearly teaches that this is not the case. What it does
mean is that the physical universe is not excluded
from the effects of redemption, as is made abundantly
plain in another glorious passage:

The creation waits in eager expectation for the
sons of God to be revealed. For the creation
was subjected to frustration, not by its own
choice, but by the will of the one who subjected
it, in hope that the creation itself will be liber-
ated from its bondage to decay and brought
into the glorious freedom of the children of

God. We know that the whole creation has been groaning as in the pains of childbirth right up to the present time. Not only so, but we ourselves, who have the firstfruits of the Spirit, groan inwardly as we wait eagerly for our adoption as sons, the redemption of our bodies. [15]

The consummation of world history to which the Christian looks forward includes the resurrection of the body. Therefore there must be an environment suitable for the renewed redeemed man, and this is exactly what the Bible teaches. There will be a new universe, a new heavens and new earth. However, some argue on the basis of some biblical passages that the present universe will be totally annihilated - destruction by fire in 2 Peter 3.10-13 is often quoted in this regard.

However, in the context Peter has been comparing the destruction of the world at the end with the destruction of the world at the time of the Flood. Now the Flood did not annihilate the earth. It cleansed and transformed the earth. Similarly, on the analogy of the resurrection body, the indications are that the new universe will be this universe transformed. The resurrection body of Jesus is his own physical body. It still bears the marks of crucifixion. It is gloriously transformed, but it is the same body. All this is tremendously important, because there have been those both within and outside the Christian church who have thought that the biblical emphasis on the end of the world means that how we treat the earth now is unimportant. By contrast, the biblical teaching is that just as Christians are to treat their bodies with respect because they are created by God, indwelt by the Holy Spirit and are one day to be resurrected, so we are to treat the creation with respect because it too is created by God, sustained by Jesus Christ and will one day be transformed. That is why Peter spoke of the end of the world as God's restoring all things. [16]

Healing Dominion

There is one final theological emphasis we discover in the Bible that is of significance for a Christian view of the earth. It is the emphasis on Christ being the representative man, not only in terms of redemption, but also in terms of dominion and headship. We have already seen the emphasis on man's dominion over creation in Genesis 1. That dominion is reiterated in Psalm 8 and it is this latter passage that is quoted in Hebrews 2 in a quite breathtaking passage in which the writer is establishing the uniqueness of Jesus Christ:

It is not to angels that he has subjected the world to come, about which we are speaking. But there is a place where someone has testified:

"What is man that you are mindful of him,
    the son of man that you care for him?
You made him a little lower than the angels;
    you crowned him with glory and honour
    and put everything under his feet."

In putting everything under him, God left nothing that is not subject to him. Yet at present we

119

do not see everything subject to him. But we see Jesus who was made a little lower than the angels, now crowned with glory and honour because he suffered death, so that by the grace of God he might suffer death for everyone. [17]

The key part of this passage is 'Yet at present we do not see everything subject to him. But we see Jesus ...' The point is that the proper dominion given to the human race at creation was so impaired by the Fall as to cease to be comprehensive, but now that proper and comprehensive dominion is restored in Jesus Christ. This is one of several passages that see Jesus as the Second Adam, the new representative man. [18] But the emphasis of this passage is that Jesus has assumed the rule over creation originally given to Adam. The Apostle Paul makes a similar point when he says of Jesus that, 'God placed all things under his feet and appointed him to be head over everything for the church, which is his body, the fulness of him who fills everything in every way.' [19]

The impact of all this upon a Christian view of ecology is that our treatment of the earth cannot be seen in isolation from our relationship with Jesus Christ. All our dealing with other creatures must be seen in the light of the truth that Christ is the Lord of the whole of life. The way we treat the earth must be defined by the characteristics of Christ's ministry. He came to save, to heal and to transform from one degree of glory to another. How incongruous it would be if in his name we tried to justify the rape, pillage and destruction of creation! Instead, we are committed by our allegiance to him to the healing of the ravages of sin upon the earth as well as upon human beings.

References

1. R. C. Zaehner, *Our Savage God: the perverse use of eastern thought*, (Sheed and Ward, 1974), ps. 71-72, quoted by John Drane in *What is the New Age saying to the Church?* (Marshall Pickering, 1991), p. 129

2. Genesis 9.6, 1 Corinthians 11.7, James 3.9

3. Matthew 10.31, 12.12

4. Genesis 6.5, Jeremiah 17.9, Romans 3.10-18, Ephesians 2.1-3

5. Genesis 2.17

6. See Luke 10.18, 2 Peter 2.4, Jude 6, Ezekiel 28.12-17, Isaiah 14.12-14, Revelation 12.7-9

7. John Lilly, *The Centre of the Cyclone: An Autobiography of Inner Space*, (Julian Press, 1972), p. 5, quoted by James Sire, op.cit., p. 189

8. Genesis 3.17-19

9. John Drane, op.cit., ps. 130,164

10. See Genesis 12.1ff, 15.1-21, 17.7,8, 22.18

11. See Meredith Kline, *The Treaty of the Great King* (1963)

12. Christopher Wright, *Living as the People of God*, (IVP, 1983), p. 59

13. Proverbs 12.10, see also Leviticus 25, Exodus 23.10-12, Deuteronomy 20.19,20(AV), 22.1-10, 5.14, Leviticus 19.19

14. Colossians 1.15-20

15. Romans 8.19-23

16. See Revelation 21.1, 2 Peter 3.3-13, John 20.24ff, 1 Corinthians 6.19,20, 15.35ff, Acts 3.21

17. Hebrews 2.5-9, see also Genesis 1.26-28 and Psalm 8

18. See 1 Corinthians 15.20-28, Romans 5.12-19

19. Ephesians 1.22,23

CONCLUSION:
NEW AGE OR NEW CREATION?

We have come a long way from the hills of South India
and of Northern Scotland through the Gates of Eden
to the Promised Land. What have we learned on our
journey? I hope we have learned many things. I hope
we have learned that nothing in life is as simple as it
may at first appear. Ecology is not simple. That is
because God has created a complex earth where each
creature is dependent on others and we are all ultimately dependent on him. It is so typical of New Age
Man to mistake the process God has created, and by
which he sustains the world, with Deity itself and
worship it as Gaia. But the Christian does not deny
the complexity of the process. Indeed, he sees it as
being so complex that it is beyond the unaided wit of
man to comprehend it and control it.

I hope we have learned too that the ecological
crisis is a crisis not only because the actual physical,
chemical and biological processes which have led to
the present state of affairs are complex, but also
because the decisive role of man has too often been
dominated by the destructive mixture of man-centred
thinking and a perverted love of power and wealth.
Certainly twentieth century science and technology

have been so dominated. This is very far from saying that science and technology in themselves are evil. They were originally built on a Christian base and have given us so many blessings not least in medical treatment. Those who decry science and technology would thank God for them if they needed anaesthetic and major surgery after a road accident. However, we see in ecology as in every other area of life that there is an intractable problem in the heart of man - the problem of sin. We have a crisis not because we are not yet highly enough evolved, nor because we have forgotten we are divine, but because we are rebels against God who created us.

This is where New Age thinking fails. Like all man-centred thought, it refuses to accept the fact of human guilt and sin. Dylan expressed this powerfully in 1965 in his visionary song 'Gates of Eden'. Within the Gates of Eden was the perfect environment we all long for. But at that stage he thought that not only would there be no sins and no guilt there, but also no distinctions between the real and the non-real.[1] If the price we pay for denying the existence of sin is the simultaneous denying of reality, then we are truly bankrupt. We have no firm place to stand to condemn any action, even the despoiling of the earth.

Again, New Age thinking was clearly foreseen by C. S. Lewis in *Perelandra*, the second book of his science fiction trilogy. In this second novel the scientist Weston describes how he has undergone a conversion from humanism to what would now be called New Age thinking. He is now a 'materialist magician':

I saw almost at once that I could admit no break, no discontinuity, in the unfolding of the cosmic process. I became a convinced believer in emergent evolution. All is one. The stuff of mind, the unconsciously purposive dynamism, is present from the very beginning ... Call it a Force. A great, inscrutable Force, pouring up into us from the dark bases of being. A Force that can choose its instruments ... There is no possible distinction in concrete thought between me and the universe. In so far as I am the conductor of the central forward pressure of the universe, I am it ... I am the Universe. I, Weston, am your God and your Devil. I call that Force into me completely ... [2]

From this point on Lewis describes the horrifying possession of Weston by occult forces and the destruction which he seeks to cause in the unfallen world of Perelandra. I am reminded of the words of Farsight the Eagle in Lewis's children's book, *The Last Battle*: 'There goes one who has called on gods he does not believe in. How will it be with him if they have really come?'[3] In the Christian world-view there is a real personal Devil, and the Apostle Paul warns that behind the idolatry and polytheism and pantheism of ancient Greece, there were real demons.[4] Many today in curiosity or in desperation are calling on gods they do not believe in and are discovering that they have become involved with powers that are outwith their control. As James Sire puts it:

The New Age has opened a door closed since Christianity drove out the demons from the wood, desacralised the natural world and generally took a dim view of excessive interest in the affairs of Satan's kingdom of fallen angels. Now they are back, knocking on university dormroom doors, sneaking around psychology laboratories and chilling the spines of Ouija players. Modern folk have fled from grandfather's clockwork universe to great-great-grandfather's chamber of gothic horrors. [5]

Far from restoring a right attitude to creation, this neo-paganism is re-introducing the power that is most inimical to all the good works of God, including nature as well as human beings. It is of no relevance (and it is also debatable) to say that ancient paganism was less destructive to nature than the modern world is. The point is that they did not have the scientific and technological means at their disposal to dominate the world which modern man now has. The driving force of the occult is a desire for power, and the prospects for the world, if 'materialist magicians' have their way, are truly frightening.

Lest it be thought that New Age ideas are the fondly held notions of some lunatic fringe to modern society, let me stress that New Age thinking has entered into the bloodstream of our national life. The heir to the throne, the Prince of Wales, clearly holds such views:

> I am no philosopher, but I can try to explain what I feel spirit to be. It is that sense, that overwhelming experience or awareness of a one-ness with the natural world, and beyond that with the creative force that we call God which lies at the central point of all ... It lies deep in the heart of mankind as if some primeval memory. It is both pagan and Christian. [6]

Children too are well exposed to such ideas. On Saturday morning children's TV, 'Captain Planet and the Planeteers' avert one global disaster or another under the direction of the goddess-like figure Gaia, the 'Spirit of the World'.

It is time that Christians got their act together and started showing the Biblical basis for a true concern for the earth. It should be apparent by now that there is no such thing as a 'Green Philosophy'. There is a choice between Humanism or New Age or Christianity. The question is: which world-view gives a firm foundation for the right involvement of the human race in caring for the earth? It is my deep conviction that Christianity alone gives that foundation.

We need a world-view that speaks of an authority that is over man. Humanism has been wallowing for decades now in a morass of its own making, because it has no such authority. Neither does New Age have such an authority. Although it speaks of a new spirituality, that spirituality is ultimately reduced to the impersonal process of the universe or to shadowy spirits or forces who have only ever enslaved human beings to ignorance, folly and cruelty. We need to rediscover the personalness of the Creator who stands as an authority over man scrutinising all that we do and to whom we are answerable. We need too the emphasis of Christianity that at once stresses the transcendence and the immanence of God. The universe is both distinct from him and dependent upon him. Nature is not to be confused with God so that we are afraid to explore it, use it and control it lest we are being sacrilegious. Neither is nature to be seen as something of no concern to God in order that we can use it or destroy it as we see fit.

Equally we need the dual emphasis of the Bible on the dominion and the fallenness of man. Apart from the fact that God has given us the task of caring for the earth, we have no right to interfere with nature. But unless we remember that we are fallen we will have neither a coherent explanation of why the world is abnormal, nor an adequate curb on our pride. In addition we need to know that God has acted decisively to deal with human sin and to redeem the creation. Only the real space-time death of Jesus Christ on the cross deals with the evil in the human heart. Only by his power can there be a radical transformation in our attitude from being self-centred to being God-centred. Only thus is there hope for a better treatment of the creation as those who trust in Christ seek to follow the teaching of his Word. This includes not only the practical counsel concerning care for creation which we have already noted, but also compassion for our fellow human beings. So many ecological disasters threaten the well-being of humans as well as that of animals, and one of the primary commands of Jesus is to love our neighbours as we love ourselves. So it is wrong for any group of mankind to act in such a way that the livelihood or even the life of others is harmed. Similarly it is wrong for one generation to exhaust resources so as to leave the next generation impoverished.

Above all, we need the Biblical emphasis that God has not abandoned the earth to evil. He is Lord of the earth and Christ has reconciled the whole creation to God. Yes, the day will come when the universe is transformed and purified, but there will also be continuity between the present heavens and earth and the new heavens and earth. Thus it matters eternally how we care for the earth.

References

1. Bob Dylan, 'Gates of Eden', in *Lyrics*: 1962-1985, (Jonathan Cape, 1987), p. 175
2. C. S. Lewis, *Perelandra*, (Pan Books, 1983), ps. 81,83,86
3. C. S. Lewis, *The Last Battle*, (Puffin Books, 1964), p.106
4. 1 Corinthians 10.20
5. James Sire, *The Universe Next Door*, (IVP, 1988), p.204
6. *Press and Journal*, 31 January 1992